the magic of ORIGAMI

the magic of origami

by Alice Gray and Kunihiko Kasahara
with Cooperation of Lillian Oppenheimer
and Origami Center of America

 japan publications, inc.

© 1977,1985 in Japan by Japan Publications, Inc.

Published by
JAPAN PUBLICATIONS, INC., Tokyo & New York

Distributors:
UNITED STATES: *Kodansha America, Inc., through Farrar, Straus &
Giroux, 19 Union Square West, New York, N.Y. 10003.* CANADA: *Fitzhenry
& Whiteside Ltd., 195 Allstate Parkway, Markham, Ontario, L3R 4T8.*
BRITISH ISLES AND EUROPEAN CONTINENT: *Premier Book Marketing Ltd.,
I Gower Street, London WC1E 6HA.* AUSTRALIA AND NEW ZEALAND
*Bookwise International, 54 Crittenden Road, Findon, South Australia
5023.* THE FAR EAST AND JAPAN: *Japan Publications Trading Co., Ltd.,
1–2–1, Sarugaku-cho, Chiyoda-ku, Tokyo 101.*

First edition: June 1977
Revised paperback edition: September 1985
Seventh printing: August 1993

ISBN 0–87040–390–7
LCCC No. 77–74654

Printed in U.S.A.

Contents

About Origami in General and This Book in Particular, 7

First Things First
How to Read Origami Directions, 8
Origami Dictionary, 11
Paper for Folding, 16
What to Do with Origami, 17

Models Made from Rectangles
Catcher's Mitt, 18 / Nurse's Cap, 19 / Letter Fold, 20 / Letterfold or
Needle Case, 20 / Leaping Frog, 21 / Boomerang Plane, 22 / Dory, 23
Box, 24 / Furniture, 25 / Basket, 26 / Napkin Fold, 28 / Bow-tie, 30
Lovers' Knot, 31 / Ring for Finger or Napkin, 32 / Elephant, 34

Models Made from Squares
Walking Penguin, 37 / Flying Wings, 38 / Animal Head Finger Puppet,
40 / Pigeon, 42 / Nodding Bird, 43 / Dwarf, 44 / Three-piece
Ornament, 46 / Blow-top, 47 / Sea Shell, 48 / Scallop Shell, 49 / Crab,
50 / Catboat, 51 / Clown, 52 / Santa Claus, 54 / Coaster, 56 / Bride, 58
Purse or Stamp Case, 60 / Tumbler, 61 / Bed, 62 / Chair, 63 / Wall
Clock, 63 / Windmill Base, 64 / Table, 65 / Two-piece Helicopter, 66
Two-piece Windmill, 67 / Crown, 68 / The Blintz Base, 69 / Camera,
70 / Basket, 72 / Water-bomb Base and Balloon, 74 / FAceted Water-
bomb, 75 / Boxer or Tulip Flower, 76 / Stem and Leaf for Tulip, 77 Six
Water-bomb Base Ornament, 78 / How to Make an Origami Mobile,
79 / Fish Base and Fish, 80 / Valentine Letterfold, 81 / Two-piece
Alligator, 82 / Bird Base and Crane, 84 / Flapping Bird and Flapping
Crane, 86 / Pop Star, 87 / Snail, 88 / Rabbit, 90 / Frog or Lily Base, 92
Lily and Iris, 94 / Jumping Frog, 96 / Bell, 97

Christmas Tree Ornaments
How to Make a Square from an Irregular Piece of Paper, 99 / Square
Ornament with Shelves, 100 / Diamond-shaped Ornament with
Shelves, 101 / Outside-inside Ornament, 101 / Crystal Tree
Ornament, 102 Eight Vaned Tree Ornament, 103 / Stirrup
Ornament, 103 / Drop-shaped Ornament, 104 / Strawberry Ornament,
104 / Lemon-shaped Ornament, 105 / Zig-zag Tree Ornament, 106
Octahedron, 107 / Embroidered Ball, 108 / Ornamental Ball, 109
Christmas Tree (i), 110 / Christmas Tree (ii), 112

Models Made from paper of Other Shapes

How to Make an Isosceles Right Triangle from a Square, *114* Mouse, *115* / How to Make an Equilateral Triangle from a Long Rectangle or Strip, *116* / Star of David, *117* / How to Make a Regular Hexagon from a Long Rectangle or Strip, *118* / Octahedron, *119* How to Make a Regular Pentagon and Fivepointed Star from a Square, *120* / Star, *121* / How to Make a Regular Octagon from a Square, *122* / Pinwheel or Zinnia Flower, *124* / How to Make a Paper Circular, *126* / Rocking Bird, *126* / Chicken, *127* / Nun, *128* / Invent Your Own Origami, *130*

About Origami in General and This Book in Particular

"ORIGAMI" is a Japanese word. It means "the FOLDING of PAPER." We have adopted it into English because the kind of paperfolding in this book—the magical kind—first came to us from Japan. Perhaps you already know how to make paper cups, boats, and planes. That is origami.

Do you know how to make paper birds, flowers, animals and Christmas tree ornaments? This book will show you. A few of the models here are very old Japanese ones that every folder ought to know because so many other things can be made from them. The rest are new, or have appeared in books or magazines now hard to find. None of them is too hard for a new folder who pays attention to the directions.

Among paperfolders, it is good manners to tell who created each model, if you know. That is what we have done.

Models so old that nobody knows who invented them are marked "traditional." The Japanese models were chosen by Mr. Kunihiko Kasahara, who also drew all the diagrams.

The Western models were selected from the collection of the Origami Center of America in New York by Lillian Oppenheimer, Director of the Origami Center of America, and Alice Gray, who also wrote the text. Their authors, both Oriental and Occidental, have given us permission to share their works with you.

First Things First

How to Read Origami Directions

Origami directions are pictures. Each picture shows two things, what the model (the thing you are making) looks like after you have done the step before, and what you do next. The artist who drew the picture used different kinds of lines and arrows to show different things you need to know about the model.

Learn what these symbols (the lines and arrows) mean, and come back to these pages when you forget.

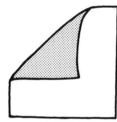

The BACK of the paper is WHITE.
The FRONT of the paper is COLORED (Screen tone).

Directions always begin with the paper back up, unless you are told otherwise.

"Valley fold"

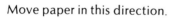

Fold upward or toward you.

⟶

Move paper in this direction.

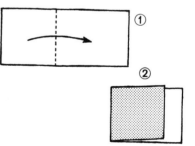

"Mountain fold"

Fold backward or away from you.

Fold back this way.

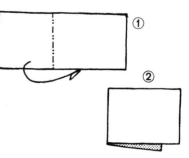

 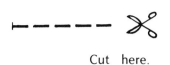 

Cut here.

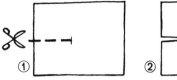

① ②

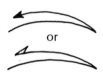

Pull. Open out.

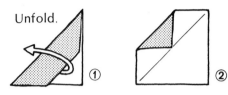

Unfold.

① ②

Turn the model over.

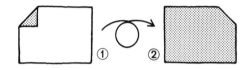

① ②

or

Fold and unfold.

① ②

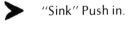

"Sink" Push in.

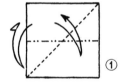 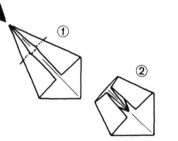

① ②

"X-ray view"
. . . .

Something that happens inside, where
you can't see it.

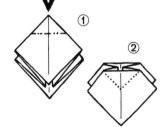 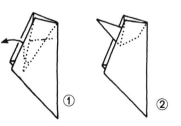

① ②

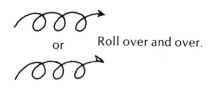 or Roll over and over.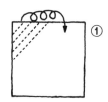

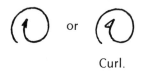 or

Curl.

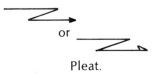 or

Pleat.

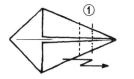

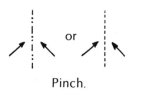 or

Pinch.

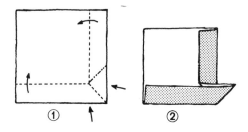

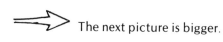 The next picture is bigger.

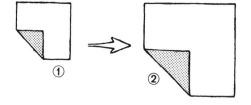

 Blow up.

See page 74 and 76 for examples.

This way to the next step. (To be used only where arrangement of plate would otherwise be confusing.)

Not all origami books use the same symbols. Whenever you use a book that is new to you, look for the symbols first. Be sure you understand them before you start to fold.

Origami Dictionary

You don't need words to read pictures: but you're going to want to teach origami and talk about it with other folders. Then you will need words—the right words. Here are a few of the most important. The words themselves you probably know already: their origami-meanings may be strange.

Most pieces of paper have EDGES and CORNERS. A square has four of each. A circle has an edge, but no corners. In origami drawings, edges are shown with HEAVY LINES.

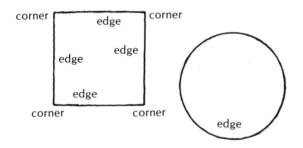

The mark made in a piece of paper by folding is a CREASE.
In drawings, a crease is shown by a very FINE LINE.

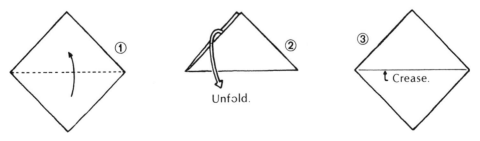

The origami thing you are making is the MODEL.

A part of the model that you can turn back and forth without moving the rest of the model is a FLAP.

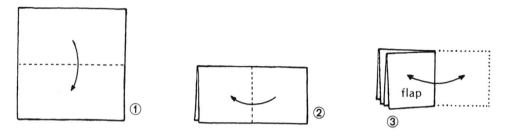

If you pinch a corner of your paper, keeping the two edges together, you will make a little flap where there was no flap before. Because of its shape, this is called a RABBIT EAR. There are other ways to make rabbit ears, and other things to make from them, but not often the ears of rabbits. Watch for them in the book.

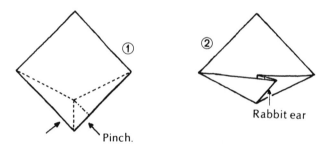

A flap usually has two layers of paper joined at one edge. If you spread the layers apart, press out the fold where they meet and push the paper down flat, you'll have two smaller flaps. This is called SQUASHING. There's a lot of squashing in this book.

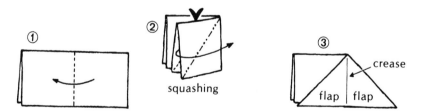

The spreading and squashing of an area that is completely enclosed, so that you cannot get a finger inside it, is called the "LOVER'S KNOT MOVE," after a traditional model in which it is used. Hard to understand, it is fun to do: the paper changes shape so amazingly as you pull. See page 31 for an example.

Many double-faced origami models are alike on both sides. To keep the sides alike when changing the direction of part of the model, you have to turn that part inside-out. This is called REVERSE FOLDING, because you reverse the directon of part of the fold at the edge of the model. If you push part of the model down between the front and back layers, you make a valley fold out of part of a mountain fold: that is an INSIDE REVERSE FOLD. If you turn a piece of the model up over the outside, front and back, you make a mountain fold out of part of a valley fold: that is an OUTSIDE REVERSE FOLD. The pictures show the difference.

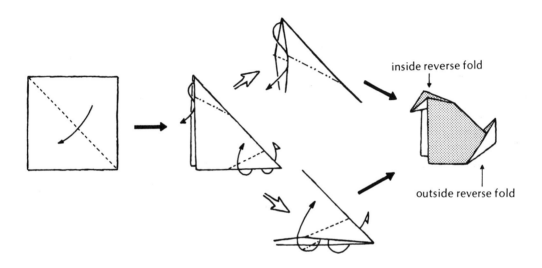

inside reverse fold

outside reverse fold

Paper folded like an accordion or a flight of steps has been PLEATED.

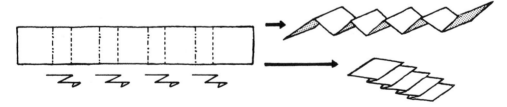

A CRIMP is a pleat at the edge of the model, but tapers to nothing at its inner end. It is used instead of a reverse fold to bend a straight edge.

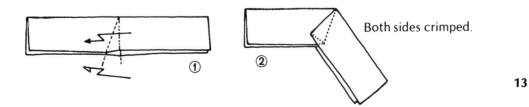

① ②

Both sides crimped.

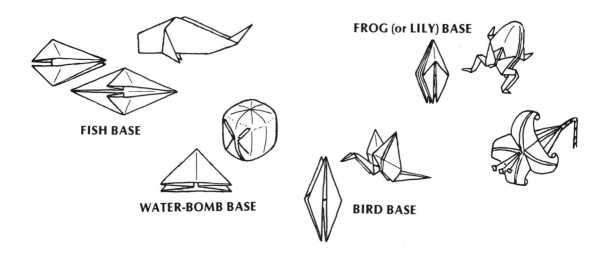

FROG (or LILY) BASE

FISH BASE

WATER-BOMB BASE

BIRD BASE

A BASE or BASIC FORM is a folded shape that doesn't look like anything but can be used to make many different models. Not all origami begins with a base, but much of it does. Each base is named after the best-known model for which it is used. When you need a base, the book will show you how to make it.

A few folded shapes even simpler than bases are used so often that they too have names. The shape is called a FOLD, and its name is a description of it.

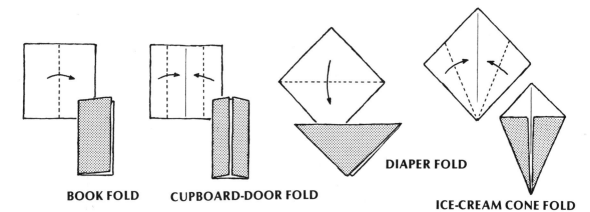

BOOK FOLD   **CUPBOARD-DOOR FOLD**

DIAPER FOLD

ICE-CREAM CONE FOLD

The PRELIMINARY FOLD is so called because several bases begin with it. (It is a Water-bomb Base turned inside out.)

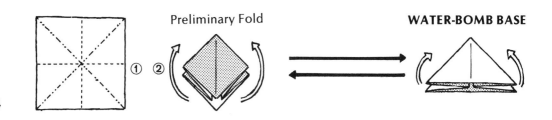

Preliminary Fold

WATER-BOMB BASE

① ②

The WING FOLD, part of the bird base, makes the wings of the bird. The PETAL FOLD, part of the frog or lily base, makes the smaller set of petals on the lily.

You will learn to make these folds when you learn the bases. They're not easy, at first, but they are so useful that you will want to make them well.

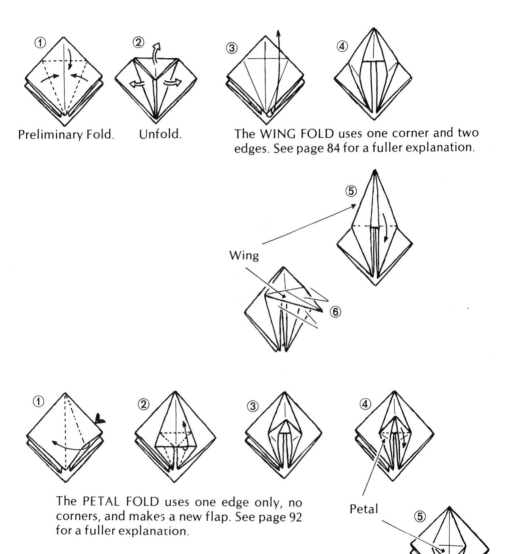

Preliminary Fold.   Unfold.

The WING FOLD uses one corner and two edges. See page 84 for a fuller explanation.

Wing

The PETAL FOLD uses one edge only, no corners, and makes a new flap. See page 92 for a fuller explanation.

Petal

Paper for Folding

Any kind of paper will do for origami, if you can fold it back and forth a few times without breaking or tearing it: but a model looks best when the paper is just right for it. A box or basket should be made of strong stiff paper. A boat or cup must be strong even when wet, and the color should not come off. Most flowers and leaves need paper the same color on both sides. If a model is many layers thick, use thin tough paper. Make Christmas tree ornaments of shiny metal foil gift-wrapping paper. Newspaper is good for hats: it is so big that the hats will fit your head.

For most origami, the paper must be square, but some models are made from rectangles the shape of this page or even longer. Some use triangles, diamond or kite shaped paper, paper five, six or eight sided, or even round.

Paper doesn't usually come in the shape you want. Often, the first step in origami is to fold the paper so that you can cut it into the right shape without having to measure anything. When you need a shape, the book will show you how to make it. Paper does usually come in sheets or rolls with parallel sides—sides the same distance apart everywhere. The directions begin with paper like that.

The size of the paper doesn't matter, unless it is so small or so large that you can't handle it. For most folding, a piece between six and twelve inches wide is good. Of course, if there is something special you want to do with the model, its size may be important. For most origami models, one sheet of paper is enough, but sometimes you will need two sheets, or even more.

The sheets may be alike or different in size, shape and color. The pieces are fitted together after folding, and may have to be glued. Sometimes you can buy packets of special Japanese origami paper in a toystore or bookshop. Brilliantly colored on one side, white on the other, it is already cut to shape—square, rectangular or round—and to different sizes. It doesn't really fold any better than notebook paper, but it is prettier, and you don't have the work of shaping it yourself.

What to Do with Origami

Origami is something you do for the fun of doing it, but the things you make are so pretty that you won't want to throw them away. Here are a few of the things you can do with them.

* Make scenes to illustrate a story or lesson.
* Decorate greeting cards and note paper.
* Make invitations, candy cups, napkin folds, place cards and hats for a party.
* Make a mobile of things that swim or fly—boats, birds or fish—as a present for a new baby.
* Make an arrangement of origami flowers in a paper vase or basket—a nice gift for Easter or for a friend in the hospital.
* Make pieces for a game.
* Make finger puppets and use them to give a short performance. (Very young children are the best audience.)
* Trim a Christmas tree.

As soon as you have learned to make a few origami models, you can teach other people to make them.
It's a good way to spend a rainy afternoon or keep busy on a long trip.

Models Made from Rectangles

You can make most of the models in this section from letter paper, newspaper or other paper that does not have to be cut to shape first. The proportions need not be very exact.

Catcher's Mitt *Traditional*

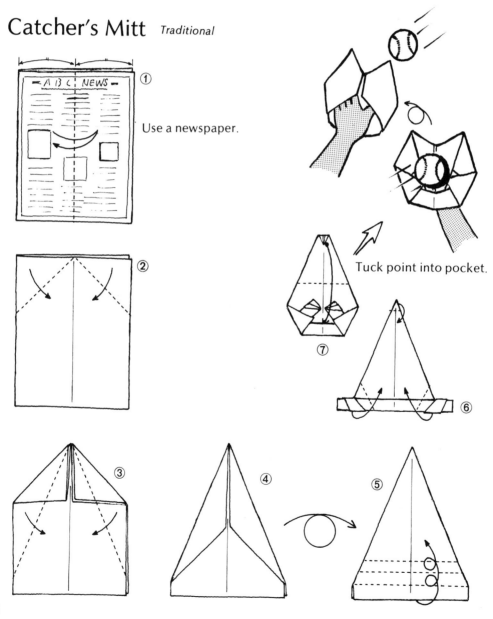

Use a newspaper.

Tuck point into pocket.

Nurse's Cap

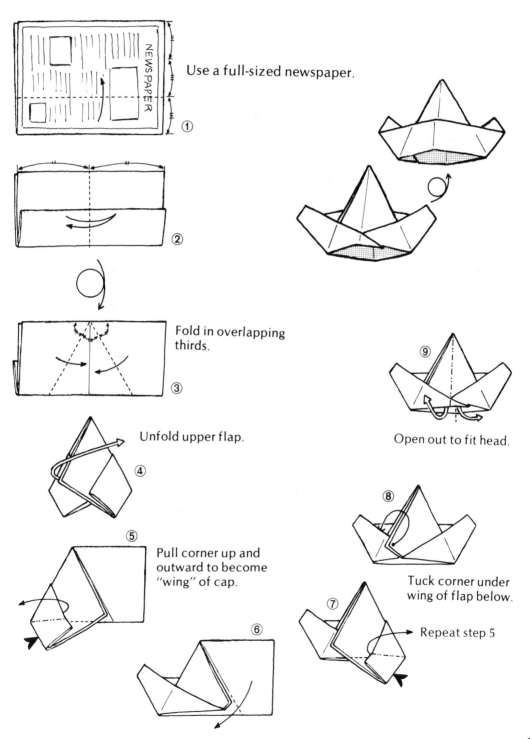

Use a full-sized newspaper.

①

②

Fold in overlapping thirds.

③

Unfold upper flap.

④

⑤ Pull corner up and outward to become "wing" of cap.

⑥

⑦

Tuck corner under wing of flap below.

Repeat step 5

⑧

⑨ Open out to fit head.

by Kunihiko Kasahara

Letterfold *Traditional*

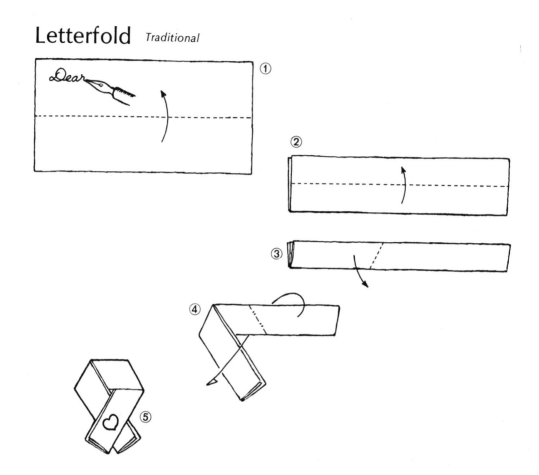

Letterfold or Needle Case

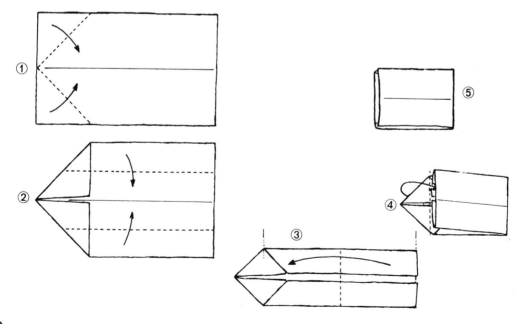

by Christopher Birch, England

Leaping Frog *Traditional*

The model is made from a standard 3″ x 5″ file card. A visiting card will do, but it is too small to be handled easily.

This frog can be used for a game. Each player tries to get his frog into a box with the fewest leaps. The box on page 24 will do, and so will the basket on page 26. You can leave off the handle.

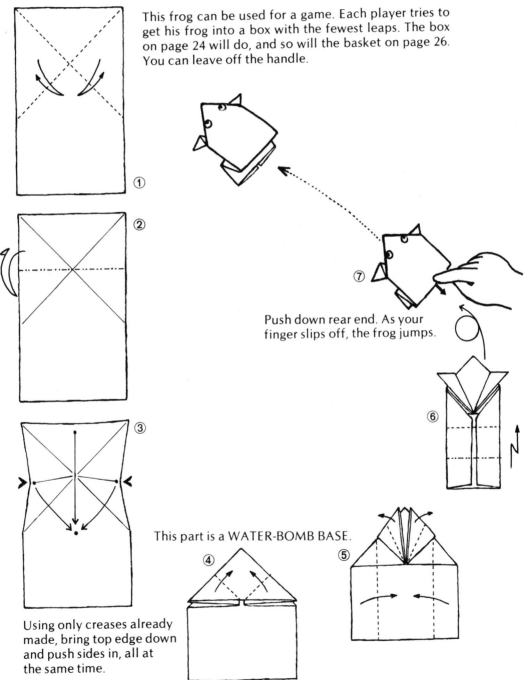

①

②

③

Push down rear end. As your finger slips off, the frog jumps.

⑦

⑥

This part is a WATER-BOMB BASE.

④

⑤

Using only creases already made, bring top edge down and push sides in, all at the same time.

Boomerang Plane

This plane makes a loop and comes back to you. It was invented by a man who got tired of chasing paper planes for a little boy in the hospital. This one he didn't need to chase.

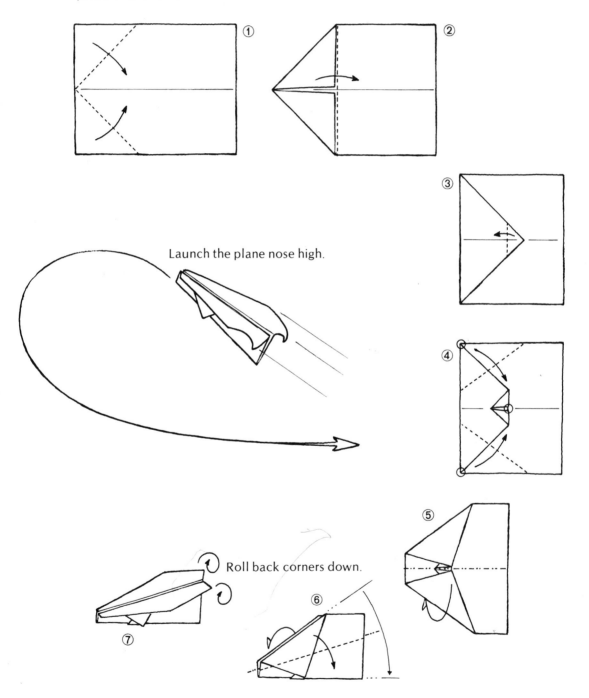

Launch the plane nose high.

Roll back corners down.

by George Jarschauer, U.S.A.

Dory
Traditional

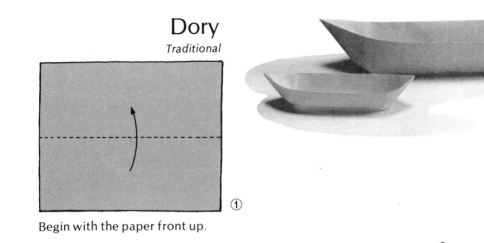

Begin with the paper front up.

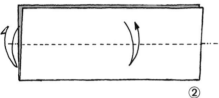

② ③

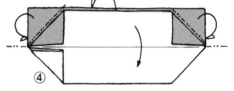

④

⑤

Spread the sides of the boat apart and push the bottom corners in with your thumb nail.

⑥

This boat really floats, but it needs something heavy in bottom to keep it right-side up.

Box

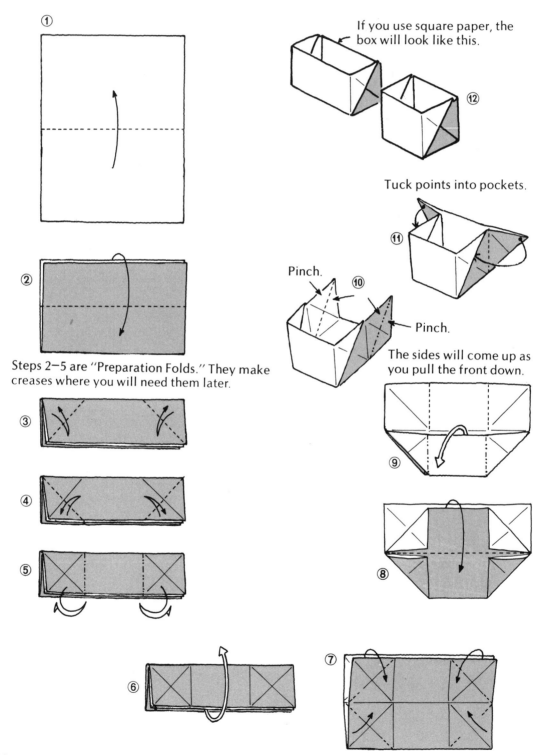

①

②

Steps 2–5 are "Preparation Folds." They make creases where you will need them later.

③

④

⑤

⑥

⑦

⑧

⑨ The sides will come up as you pull the front down.

⑩ Pinch.   Pinch.

⑪ Tuck points into pockets.

⑫ If you use square paper, the box will look like this.

by Guiseppe Baggi, Italy

Furniture

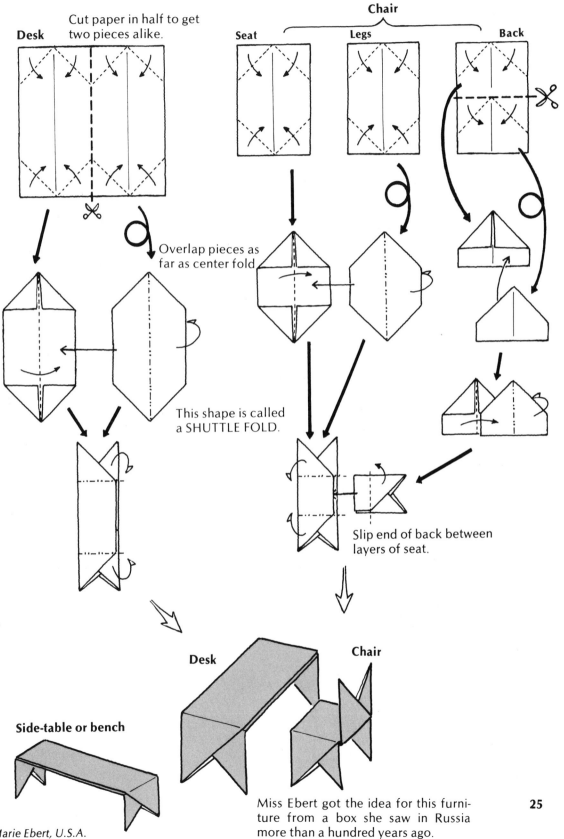

Desk

Cut paper in half to get two pieces alike.

Chair

Seat   Legs   Back

Overlap pieces as far as center fold

This shape is called a SHUTTLE FOLD.

Slip end of back between layers of seat.

Side-table or bench

Desk

Chair

Miss Ebert got the idea for this furniture from a box she saw in Russia more than a hundred years ago.

by Marie Ebert, U.S.A.

25

Basket

This basket is as strong as the paper you use.
The paper must tear before it comes apart.

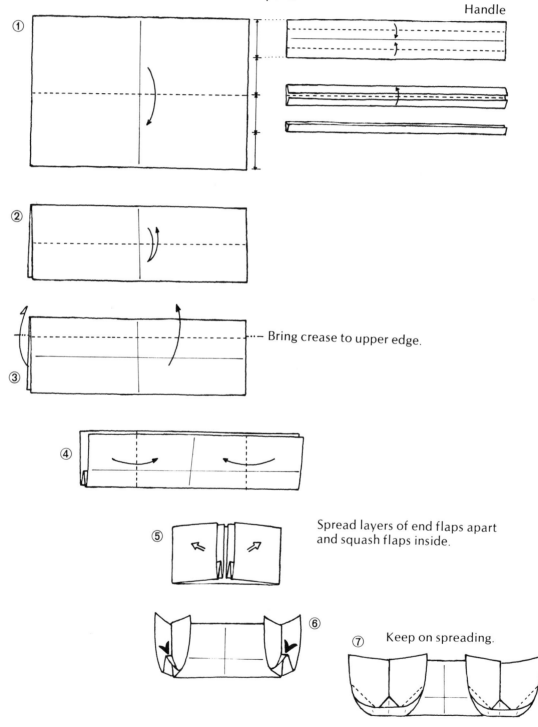

① Handle

② Bring crease to upper edge.

③

④

⑤ Spread layers of end flaps apart
and squash flaps inside.

⑥ ⑦ Keep on spreading.

by Jack Skillman, U.S.A.

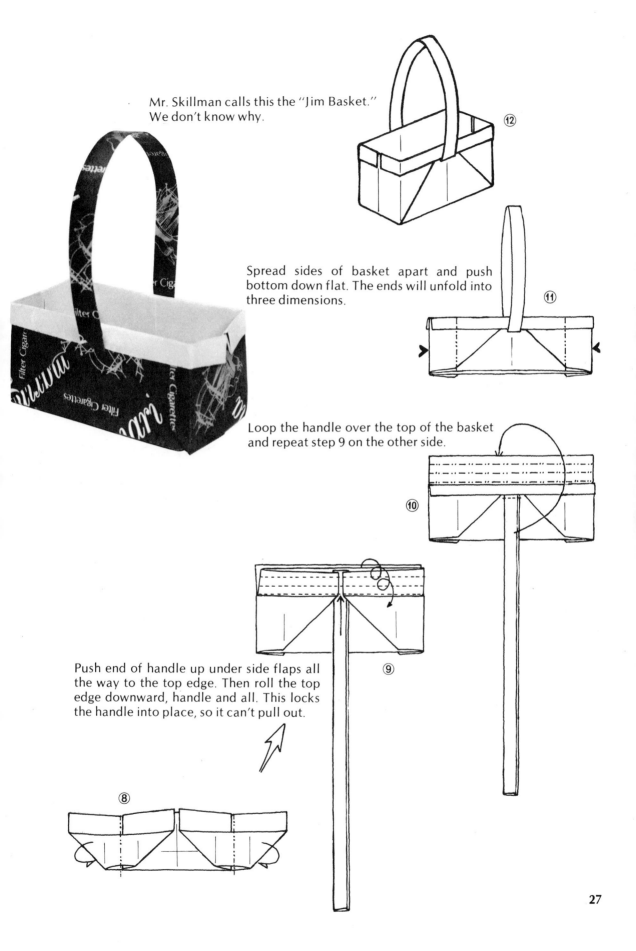

Mr. Skillman calls this the "Jim Basket."
We don't know why.

⑫

Spread sides of basket apart and push bottom down flat. The ends will unfold into three dimensions.

⑪

Loop the handle over the top of the basket and repeat step 9 on the other side.

⑩

Push end of handle up under side flaps all the way to the top edge. Then roll the top edge downward, handle and all. This locks the handle into place, so it can't pull out.

⑨

⑧

Napkin Fold (Rabbit)

Lillian Oppenheimer learned this from a visitor to the Origami Center whose name she has forgotten.

①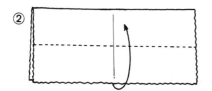

Use a cloth napkin or a big strong paper dinner napkin of a solid color.

Don't forget to fold the dinner napkins this way on Easter Sunday.

②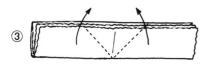

③

④

⑤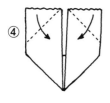

⑩

Open out the face and ears.

⑨

⑧

⑥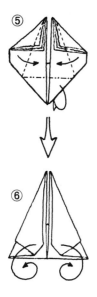

⑦

Roll bottom corners inward, overlap them and tuck one of them between the layers of the other.

Napkin Fold (Boot)

You can make this from a dollar bill too, if you first fold the bill in half lengthwise.

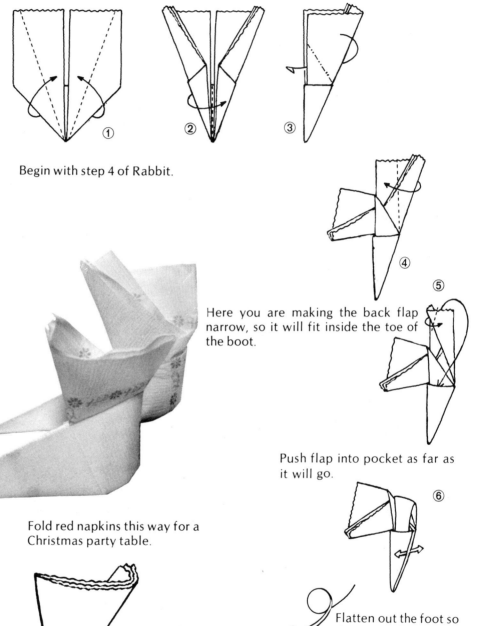

Begin with step 4 of Rabbit.

Here you are making the back flap narrow, so it will fit inside the toe of the boot.

Push flap into pocket as far as it will go.

Flatten out the foot so the boot will stand.

Fold red napkins this way for a Christmas party table.

Traditional

Bow-tie (Money fold)

Make this from a dollar bill.

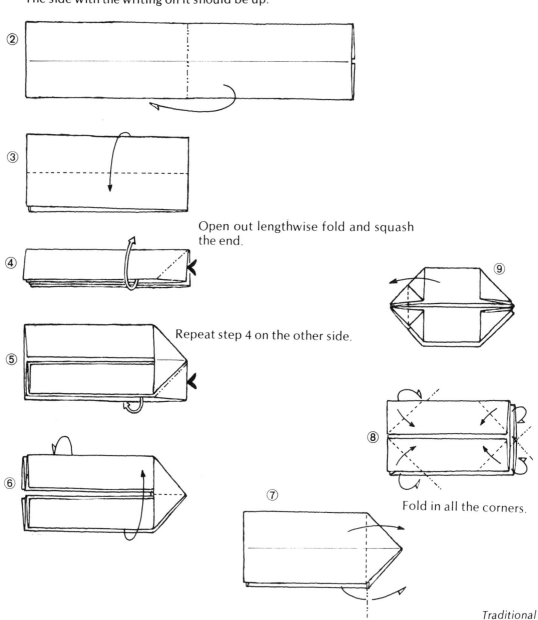

The side with the writing on it should be up.

Open out lengthwise fold and squash the end.

Repeat step 4 on the other side.

Fold in all the corners.

Traditional

Lovers' Knot

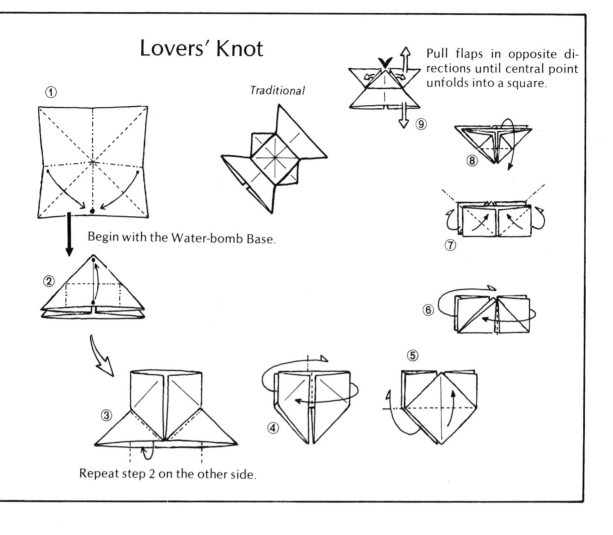

Traditional

Begin with the Water-bomb Base.

Pull flaps in opposite directions until central point unfolds into a square.

Repeat step 2 on the other side.

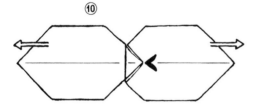

Hold on each side, as close to the center as you can, and pull. The little point in the middle will open out into a square. Pulling the sides of a flap apart to flatten it out when you can not get inside of it is called the "lovers' knot move".

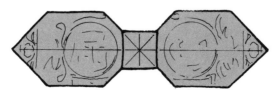

If you want to make somebody a gift of money, fold it into a Bow-tie and put it into a box. It's more fun than a plain bill in a envelope.

31

A ring made from a foil chewing-gum wrapper will fit your finger.

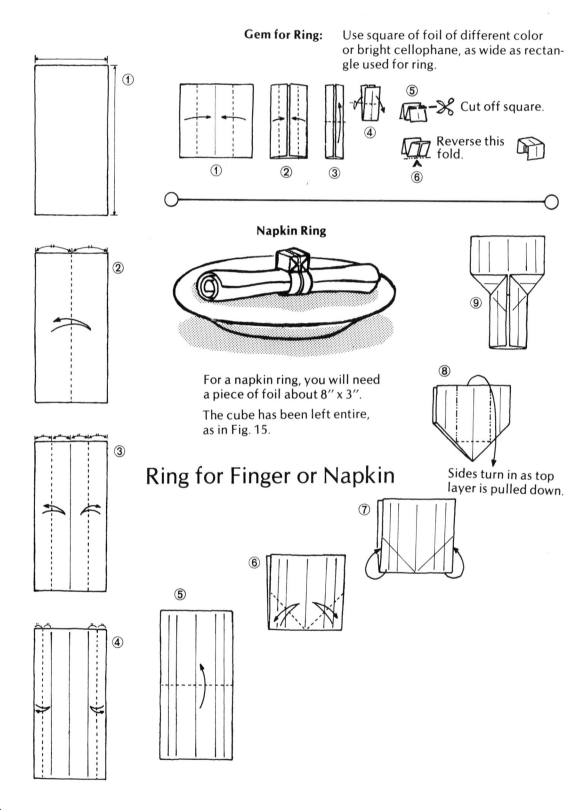

Gem for Ring: Use square of foil of different color or bright cellophane, as wide as rectangle used for ring.

⑤ Cut off square.

Reverse this fold.

Napkin Ring

For a napkin ring, you will need a piece of foil about 8″ x 3″.

The cube has been left entire, as in Fig. 15.

Ring for Finger or Napkin

Sides turn in as top layer is pulled down.

by Kunihiko Kasahara after Diamond Ring by Robert Harbin and Rolf Harris.

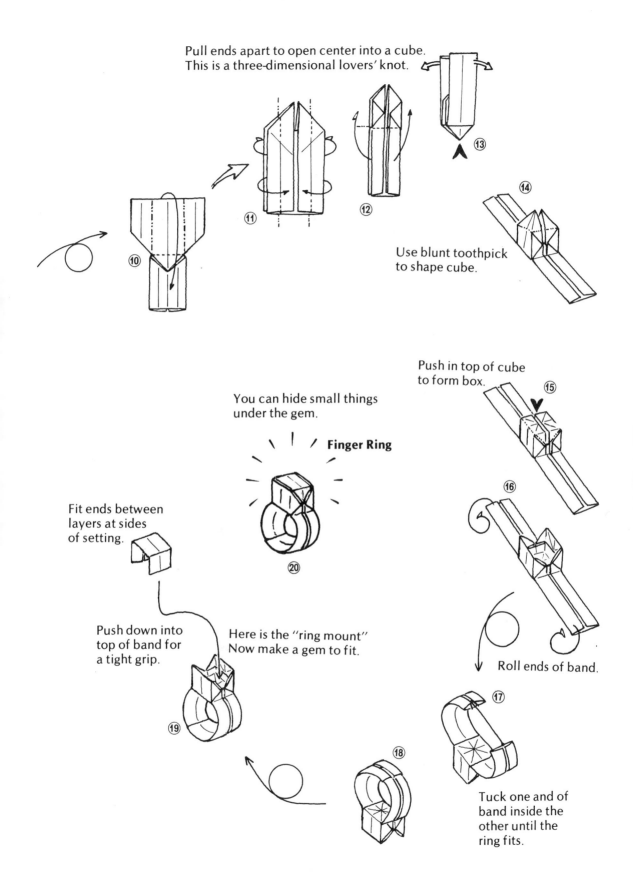

Pull ends apart to open center into a cube.
This is a three-dimensional lovers' knot.

⑬

⑭

Use blunt toothpick
to shape cube.

⑪

⑫

⑩

Push in top of cube
to form box.

⑮

⑯

You can hide small things
under the gem.

Finger Ring

⑳

Fit ends between
layers at sides
of setting.

Push down into
top of band for
a tight grip.

Here is the "ring mount"
Now make a gem to fit.

⑲

Roll ends of band.

⑰

⑱

Tuck one and of
band inside the
other until the
ring fits.

Elephant

Make this from a 2 : 1 Rectangle — half a square.

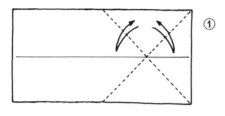

①

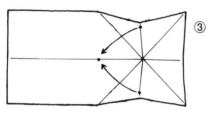

②

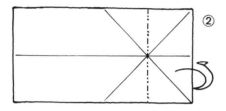

③

This part is a Water-bomb Base.

④

⑥

⑤

Pull back upper layer and
squash inner flaps.

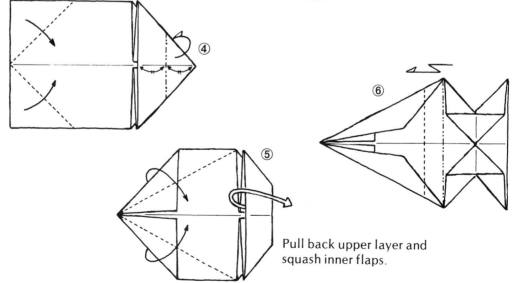

by Kunihiko Kasahara

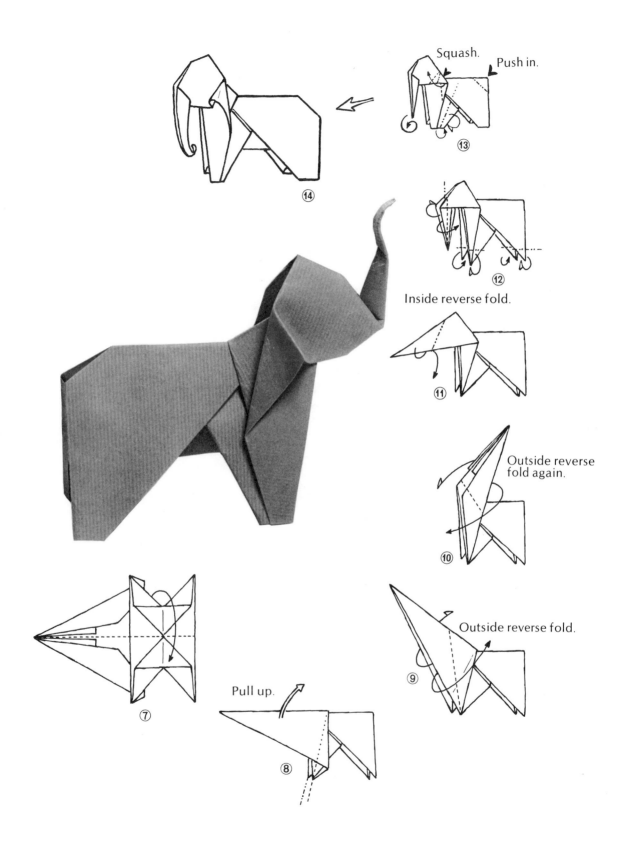

Squash. Push in.

⑬

⑭

⑫

Inside reverse fold.

⑪

Outside reverse fold again.

⑩

⑦

Pull up.

⑧

Outside reverse fold.

⑨

Models Made from Squares

More origami begins with a square than with paper of any other shape, so this is the largest section of the book. Where several models use the same "base," the base is given only once, and all the models follow it. Models that do not use a base, but do begin with the same "fold" are also close together.

If your paper is not square to begin with, you will have to cut it to shape. The best tool for cutting paper is a paper shear or photo print trimmer. There may be one at your school. Next-best is a knife with a thin blade and flat handle, a pocket knife or kitchen paring knife. The paper must be folded where you want to cut.

Hold the blade of the knife nearly parallel to the fold you are cutting, and don't saw up and down. Just push the blade along the fold, or cut on the downstroke only. Although the origami symbol for "cut" shows pair of scissors, it is not easy to cut a long straight edge with them. If you must use scissors, the longer the blades, the bettter.

TO MAKE A SQUARE from a longer rectangle, such as a sheet of writing paper.

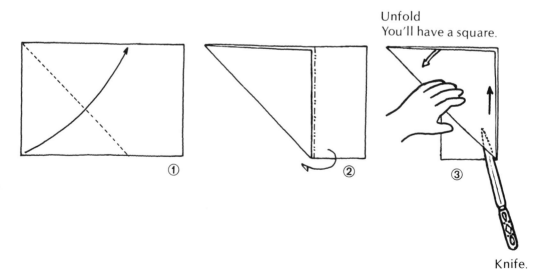

Unfold
You'll have a square.

Knife.

Walking Penguin

The paper for this model must be black on one side and white on the other.

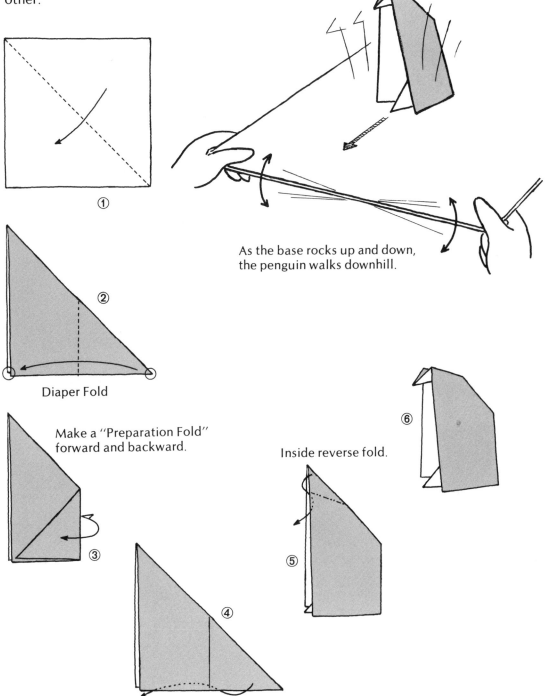

①

② Diaper Fold

Make a "Preparation Fold" forward and backward.

③

④

Make an inside reverse fold on the prepared crease.

⑤ Inside reverse fold.

⑥

As the base rocks up and down, the penguin walks downhill.

by Seiryo Takekawa, Japan

Flying Wings

Use paper 6 or 7 inches square.

①

②

③

④

⑤

⑥

Fold back a very little bit of the front edge of each wing.

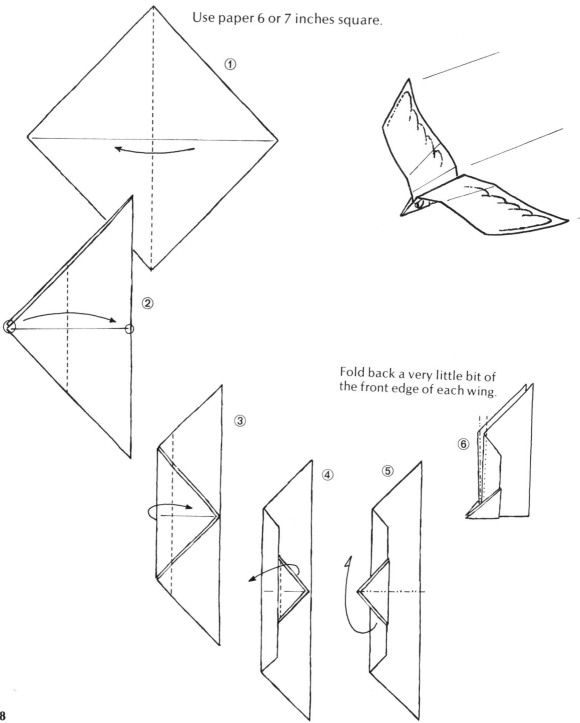

by Kunihiko Kasahara

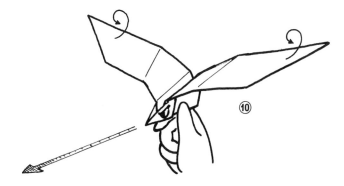

Roll tips of wings upward a little.

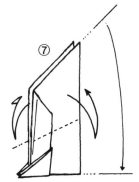

Fold and unfold.

Raise wings into flying position.

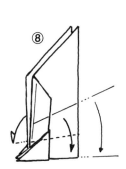

Animal Head Finger Puppet

Use paper the same color on both sides and not more than three inches square. A two-inch square will make a puppet that fits your finger tightly.

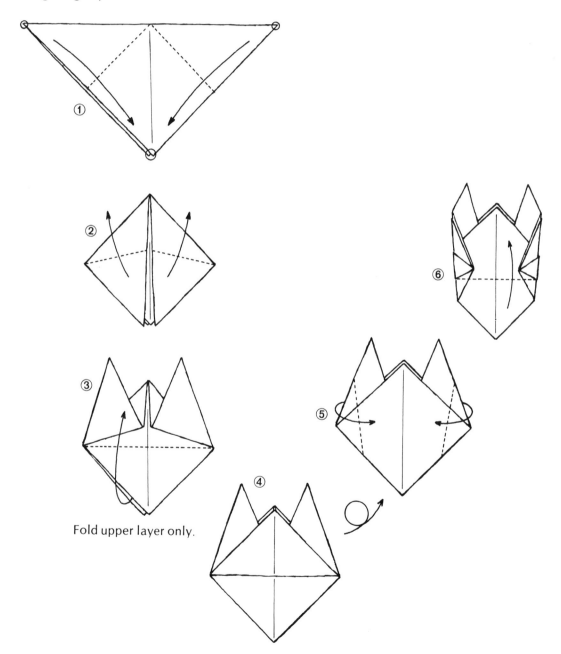

Fold upper layer only.

⑧

⑦

Fox

Dog

Here are some of the faces you can make.
Can you think of more?

Cat

Pig

Rabbit

Traditional

Pigeon

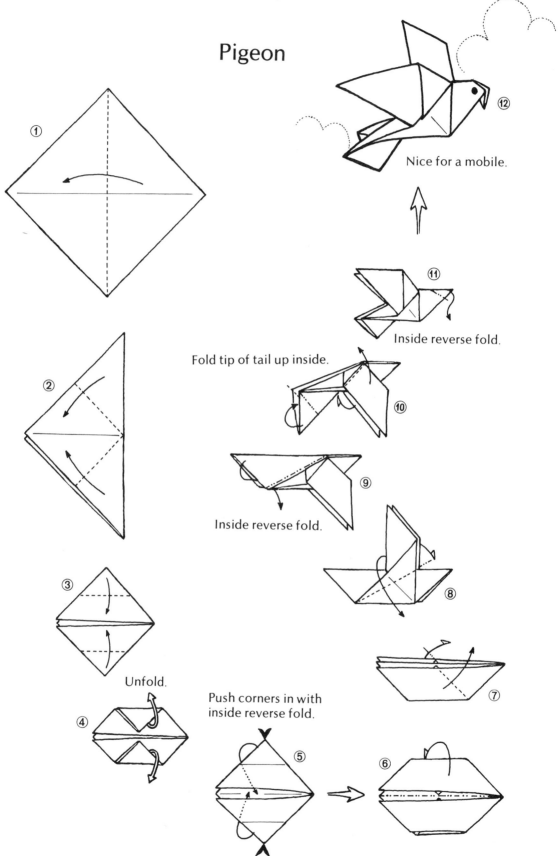

①

②

③

Unfold.

④

Push corners in with inside reverse fold.

⑤

⑥

⑦

⑧

Inside reverse fold.

⑨

Fold tip of tail up inside.

⑩

⑪

Inside reverse fold.

⑫

Nice for a mobile.

by Kunihiko Kasahara

This is prettiest when the two sides of the paper are of different colors.

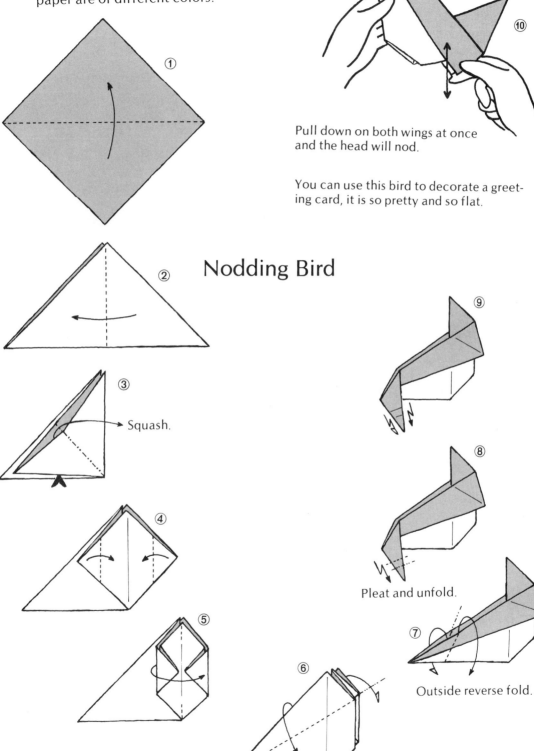

Pull down on both wings at once and the head will nod.

You can use this bird to decorate a greeting card, it is so pretty and so flat.

Nodding Bird

Squash.

Pleat and unfold.

Outside reverse fold.

by Kunihiko Kasahara

This model uses two pieces of paper the same size, colored on one side, white on the other.

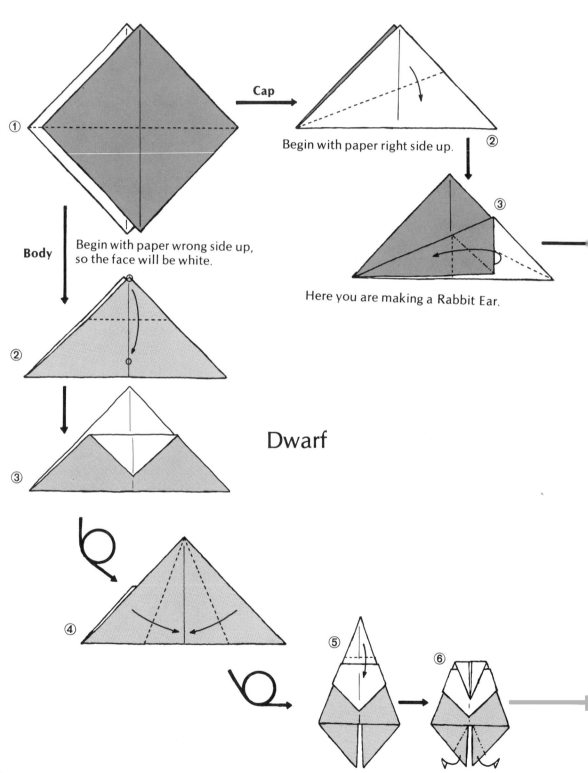

Cap

Begin with paper right side up.

Here you are making a Rabbit Ear.

Body Begin with paper wrong side up, so the face will be white.

Dwarf

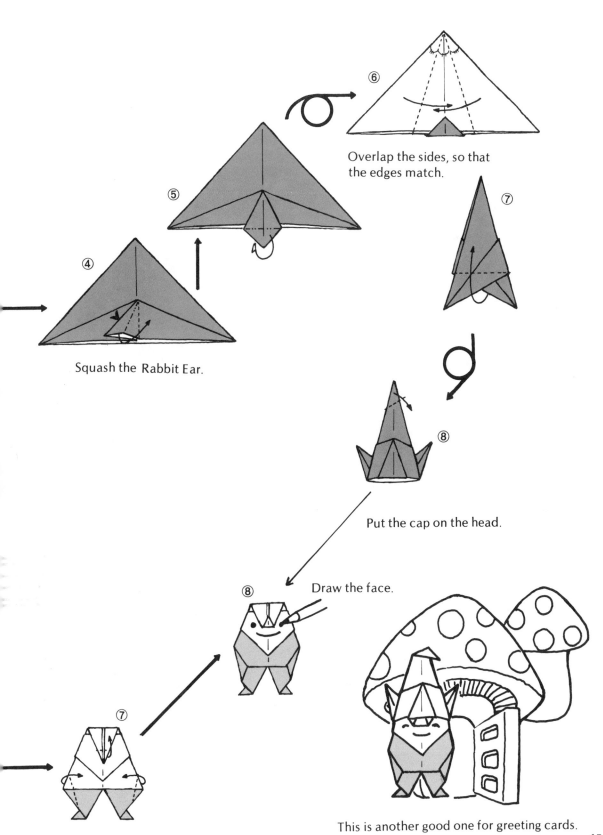

⑥ Overlap the sides, so that the edges match.

⑤

④ Squash the Rabbit Ear.

⑦

⑧ Put the cap on the head.

⑧ Draw the face.

⑦

This is another good one for greeting cards.

45

by Kunihiko Kasahara

Three-piece Ornament

A "Hexahedron", or six-sided solid.

The pieces may be of different colors. Fold all of them the same way.

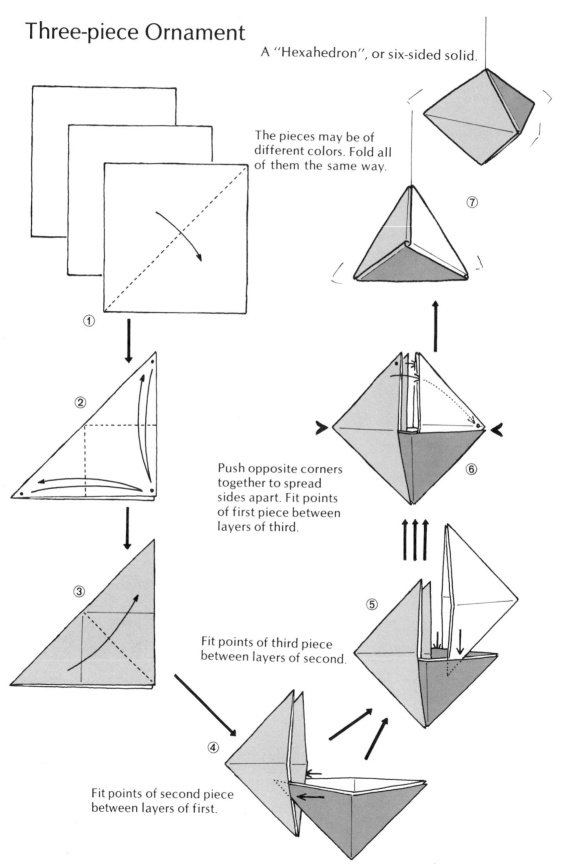

Push opposite corners together to spread sides apart. Fit points of first piece between layers of third.

Fit points of third piece between layers of second.

Fit points of second piece between layers of first.

by Molly Kahn, U.S.A.

Blow-top

3 pieces folded alike.

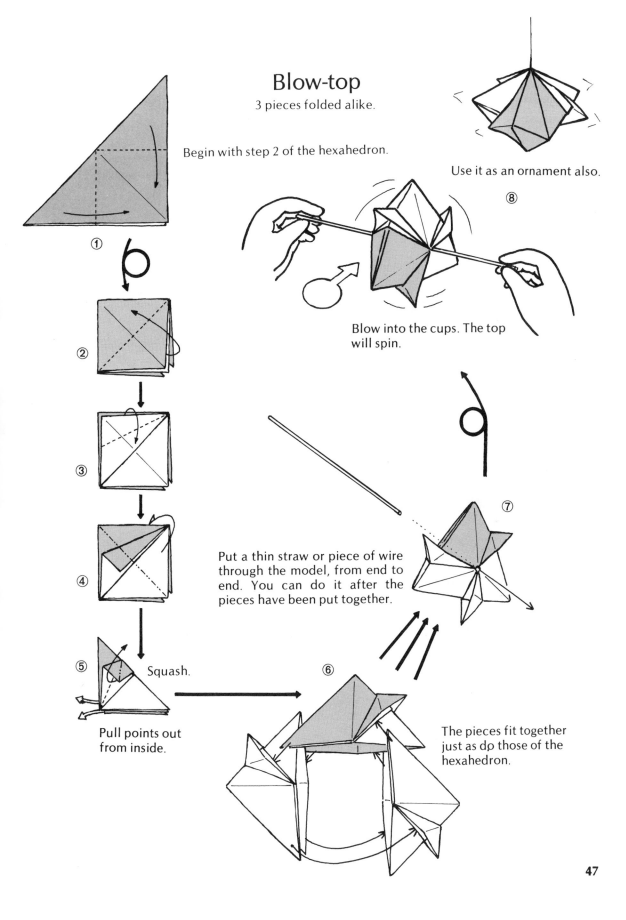

Begin with step 2 of the hexahedron.

Use it as an ornament also.

⑧

①

②

③

④

⑤

Squash.

Pull points out
from inside.

⑥

Blow into the cups. The top
will spin.

Put a thin straw or piece of wire
through the model, from end to
end. You can do it after the
pieces have been put together.

⑦

The pieces fit together
just as do those of the
hexahedron.

Use paper colored on one side only, or of different colors front and back.

The shell is three-dimensional, not flat.

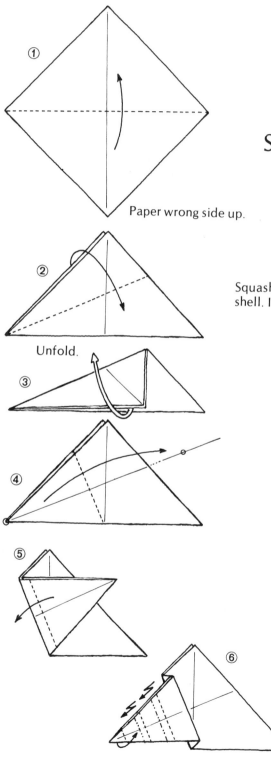

① Paper wrong side up.

② Unfold.

③

④

⑤

⑥

⑦

Sea Shell

Tip the mouth upward.

⑪

Squash, to open the mouth of the shell. It is dish-shaped.

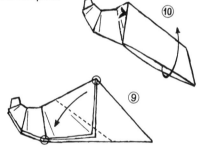

⑩

⑨

⑧

Pull each pleat upward so the bottom end opens out and the whole shell curves.

48

by Toshio Chino, Japan

Use paper the same color on both sides.

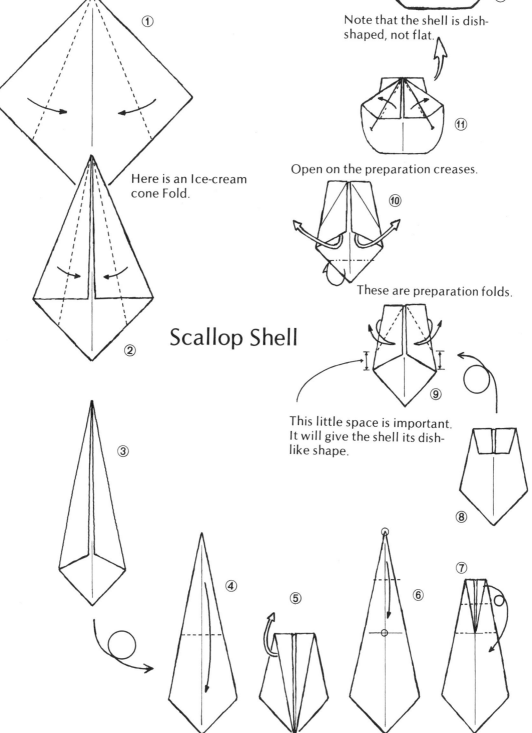

①

Here is an Ice-cream cone Fold.

②

Scallop Shell

③

④

⑤

⑥

⑦

⑧

⑨

This little space is important. It will give the shell its dish-like shape.

These are preparation folds.

⑩

Open on the preparation creases.

⑪

⑫

Note that the shell is dish-shaped, not flat.

49

by Toshio Chino, Japan

Crab

Use two sheets, different shades of the same color.

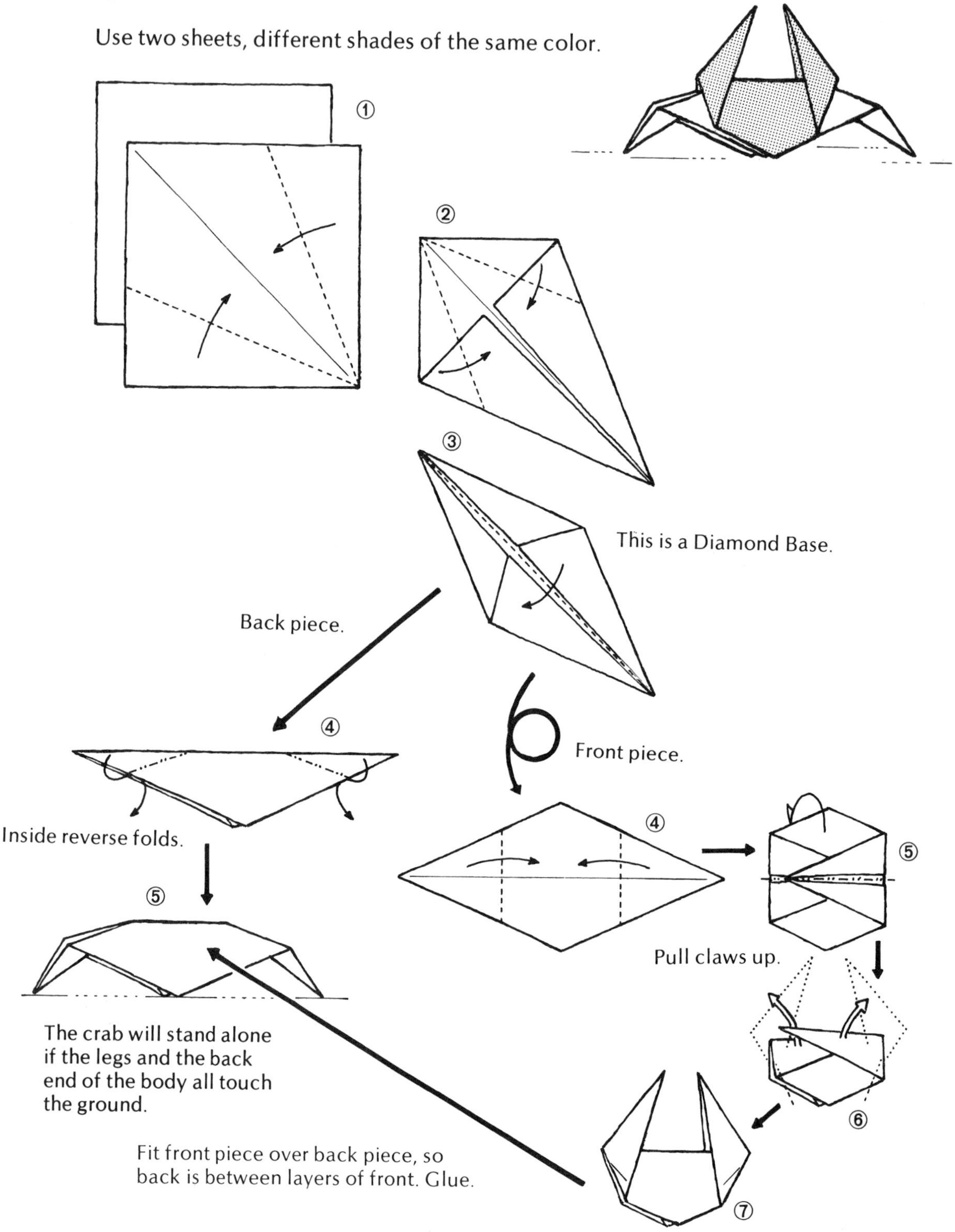

①

②

③ This is a Diamond Base.

Back piece.

④ Front piece.

Inside reverse folds.

④

⑤ Pull claws up.

⑤

The crab will stand alone if the legs and the back end of the body all touch the ground.

⑥

⑦

Fit front piece over back piece, so back is between layers of front. Glue.

by Toshio Chino, Japan

Use paper colored on one side, white on the other. Begin with the colored side up.

Catboat

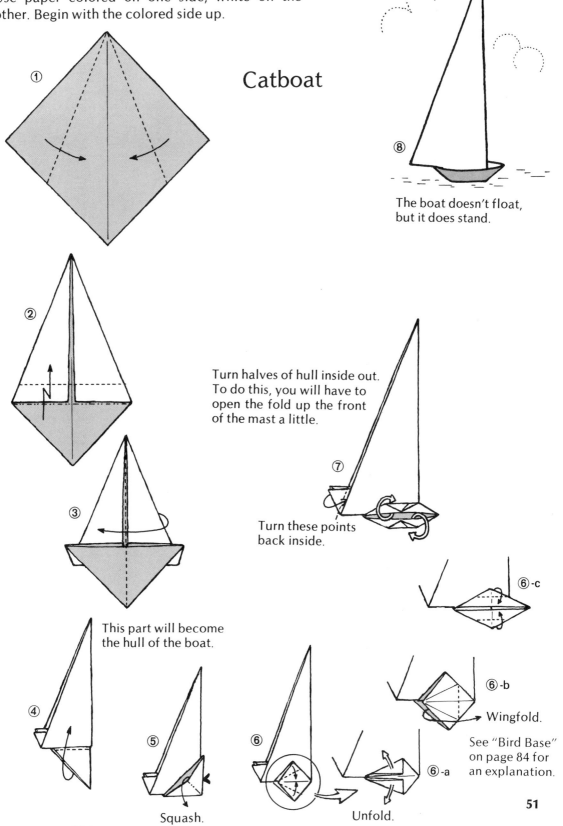

The boat doesn't float, but it does stand.

Turn halves of hull inside out. To do this, you will have to open the fold up the front of the mast a little.

Turn these points back inside.

This part will become the hull of the boat.

Squash.

Unfold.

Wingfold.

See "Bird Base" on page 84 for an explanation.

by Makoto Yamaguchi, Japan

51

Clown

Use paper colored on one side, white on the other. Begin with the colored side up.

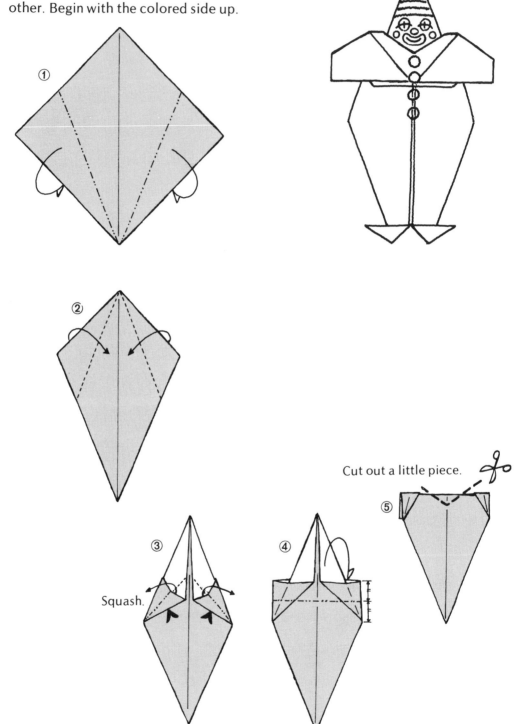

①

②

③ Squash.

④

⑤ Cut out a little piece.

after the traditional Girl's Day dolls of Japan

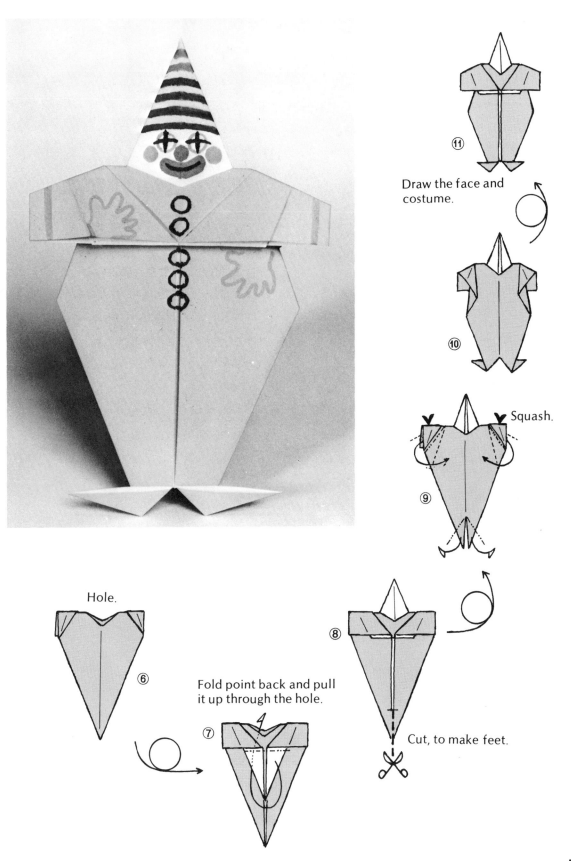

⑪

Draw the face and costume.

⑩

Squash.

⑨

⑧

Hole.

⑥

Fold point back and pull it up through the hole.

⑦

Cut, to make feet.

Santa Claus

You need two pieces of paper the same size, red on one side, white on the other.

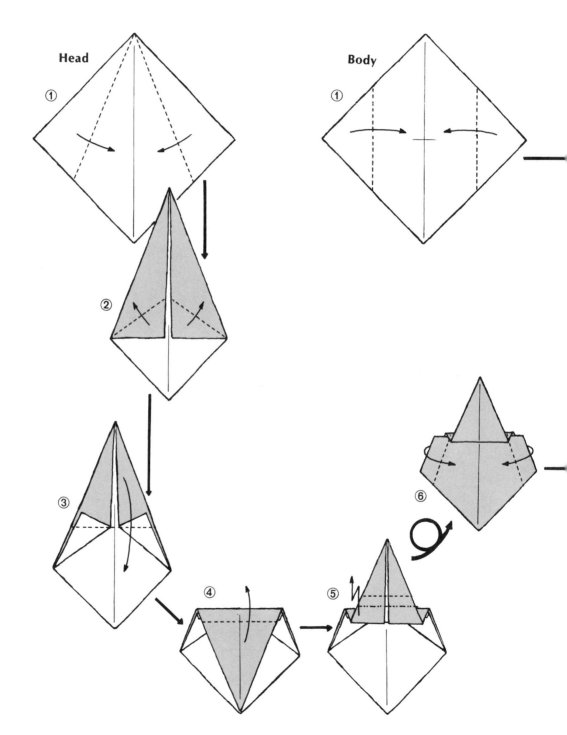

by Kunihiko Kasahara

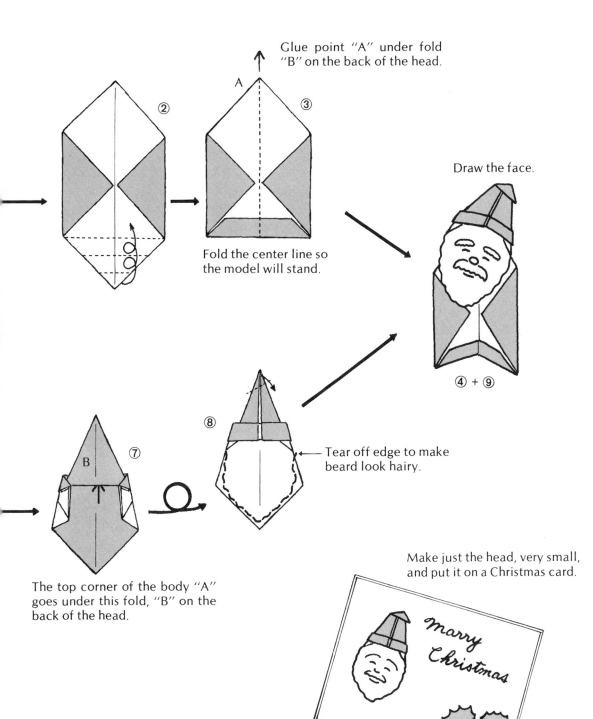

Glue point "A" under fold "B" on the back of the head.

②

③

Fold the center line so the model will stand.

Draw the face.

④ + ⑨

⑦

⑧

Tear off edge to make beard look hairy.

The top corner of the body "A" goes under this fold, "B" on the back of the head.

Make just the head, very small, and put it on a Christmas card.

Marry Christmas

This is a "modular" model—one made of many pieces alike that fit together in different ways and lock together without glue.

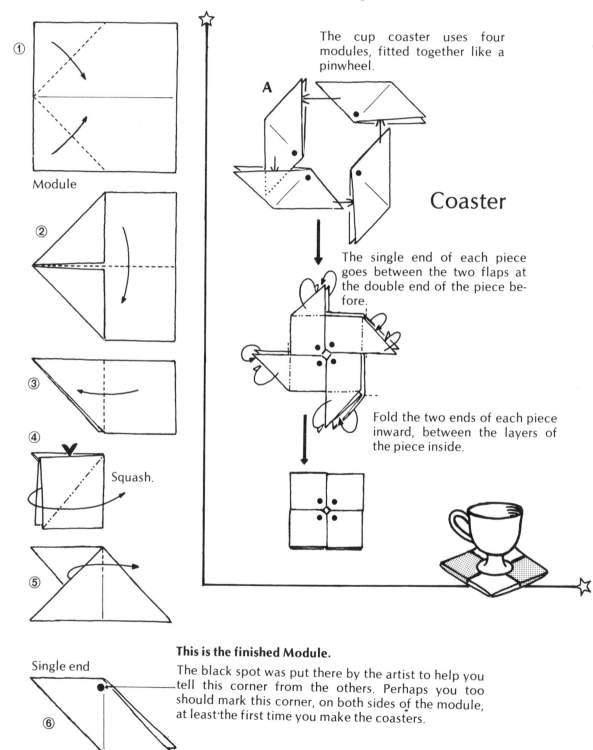

① Module

②

③

④ Squash.

⑤

⑥ Single end

Double end

The cup coaster uses four modules, fitted together like a pinwheel.

A

Coaster

The single end of each piece goes between the two flaps at the double end of the piece before.

Fold the two ends of each piece inward, between the layers of the piece inside.

This is the finished Module.

The black spot was put there by the artist to help you tell this corner from the others. Perhaps you too should mark this corner, on both sides of the module, at least the first time you make the coasters.

56

by Kunihiko Kasahara

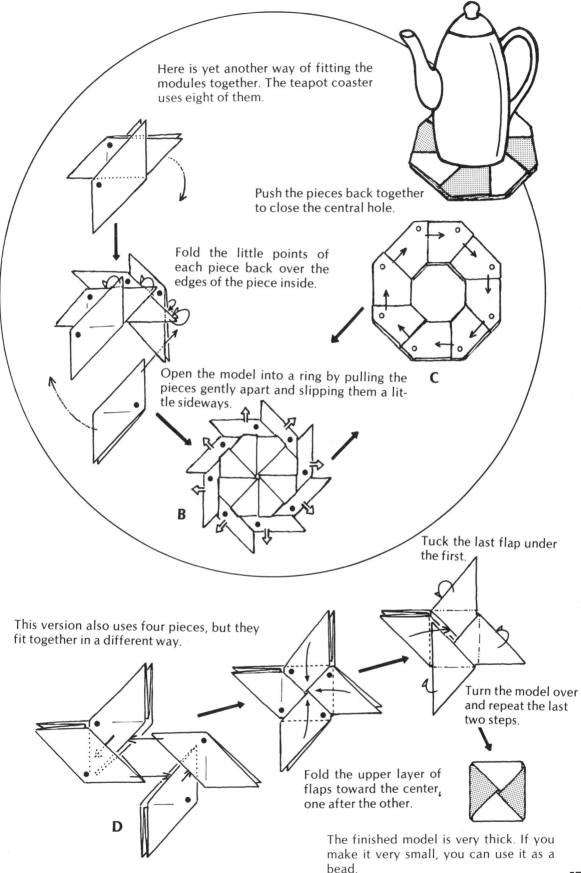

Here is yet another way of fitting the modules together. The teapot coaster uses eight of them.

Push the pieces back together to close the central hole.

Fold the little points of each piece back over the edges of the piece inside.

Open the model into a ring by pulling the pieces gently apart and slipping them a little sideways.

C

B

Tuck the last flap under the first.

This version also uses four pieces, but they fit together in a different way.

Turn the model over and repeat the last two steps.

Fold the upper layer of flaps toward the center, one after the other.

D

The finished model is very thick. If you make it very small, you can use it as a bead.

Bride

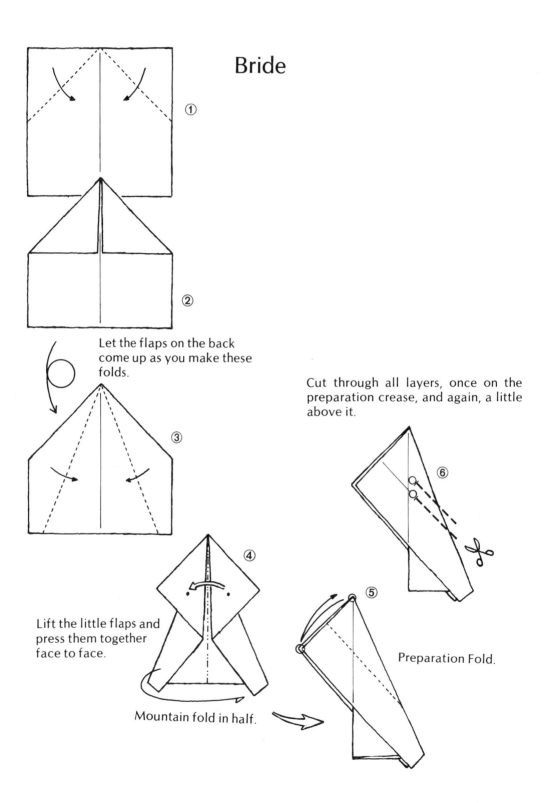

①

②

Let the flaps on the back come up as you make these folds.

③

Cut through all layers, once on the preparation crease, and again, a little above it.

⑥

Lift the little flaps and press them together face to face.

④

Mountain fold in half.

⑤

Preparation Fold.

58

by Kunihiko Kasahara

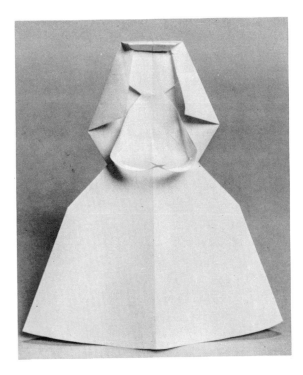

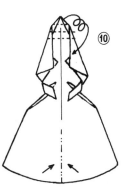

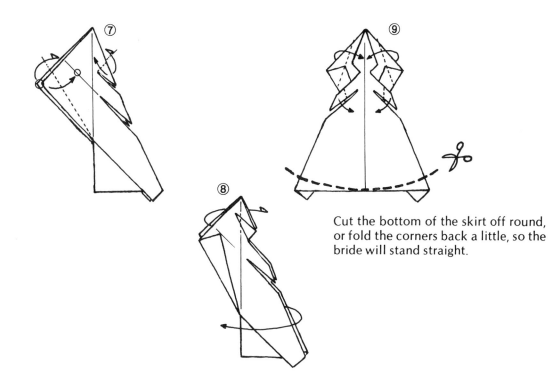

Pinch center fold of skirt.

Cut the bottom of the skirt off round, or fold the corners back a little, so the bride will stand straight.

Purse or Stamp Case

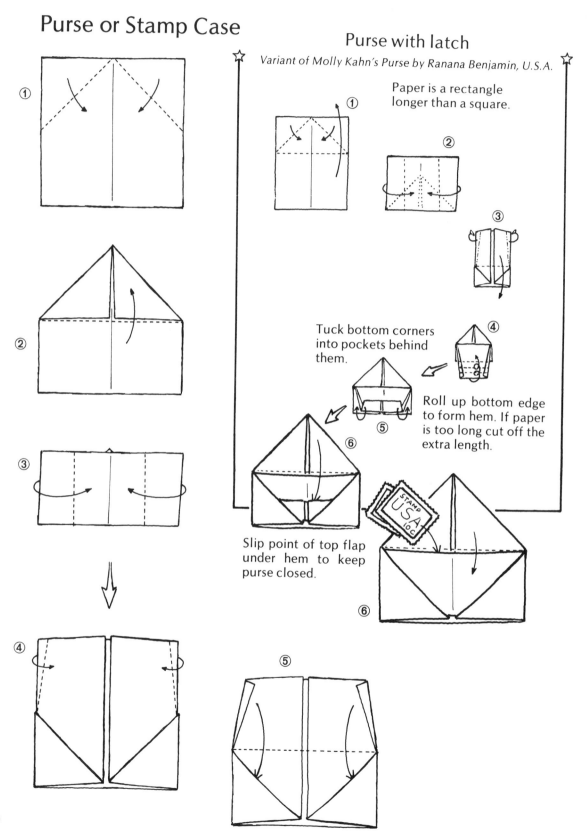

Purse with latch

Variant of Molly Kahn's Purse by Ranana Benjamin, U.S.A.

Paper is a rectangle longer than a square.

Tuck bottom corners into pockets behind them.

Roll up bottom edge to form hem. If paper is too long cut off the extra length.

Slip point of top flap under hem to keep purse closed.

STAMP USA 10c

by Molly Kahn, U.S.A.

It doesn't look like anything, but it turns somersaults.

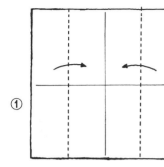 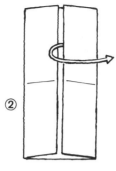 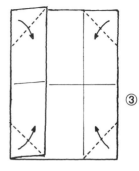

Here is a Cupboard-door Fold.

Tumbler

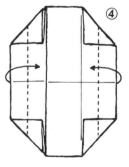

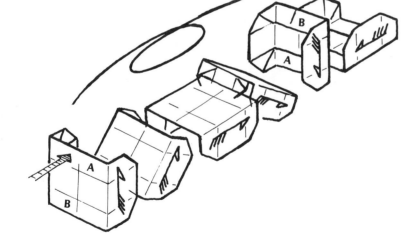

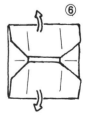

Stand the model on its thinner edge "B" on a flat surface, not slippery. It will roll over. If it doesn't, turn it around to face the other way. The surface must be sloping a little uphill.

Open sides so they stand at right-angles to the back.

61

by Seiryo Takekawa, Japan

Bed

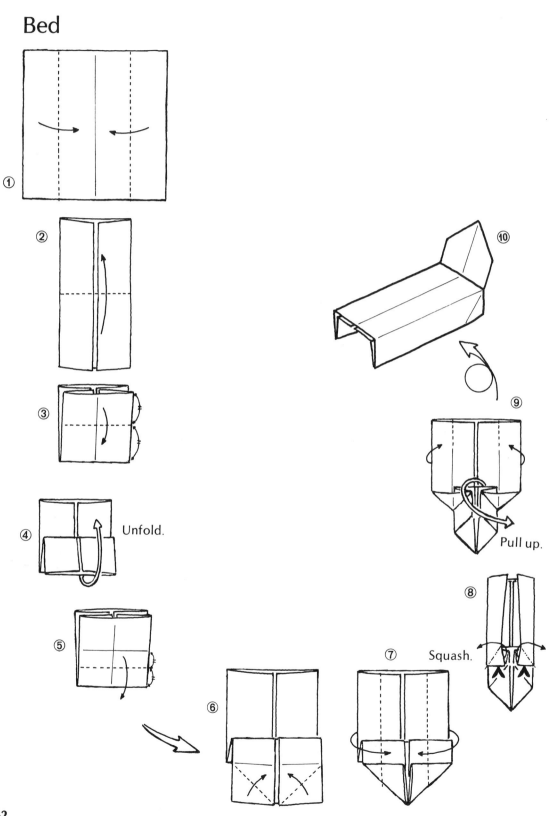

①

②

③

④ Unfold.

⑤

⑥

⑦ Squash.

⑧

⑨ Pull up.

⑩

by Taneji Nakajima, Japan

Chair

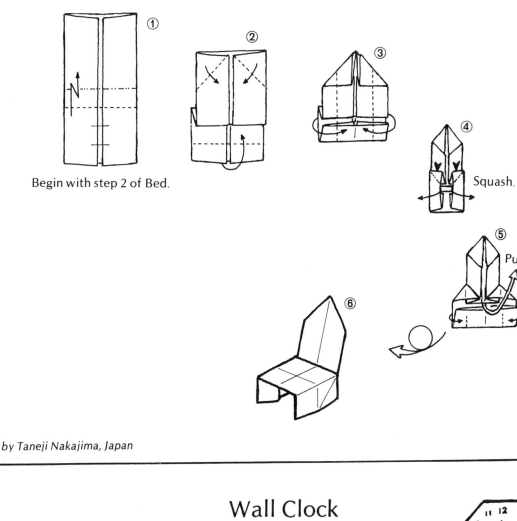

① Begin with step 2 of Bed.

②

③

④ Squash.

⑤ Pull up.

⑥

by Taneji Nakajima, Japan

Wall Clock

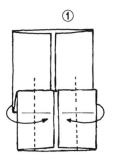

① Begin with step 6 of bed.

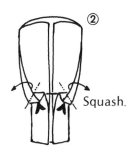

② Squash.

③

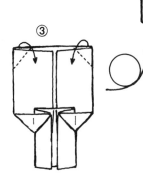

④

11 12 1
10　　　2
9　　　3
8　　　4
7 6 5

63

by Kunihiko Kasahara

Windmill Base (Pinwheel and Catamaran)

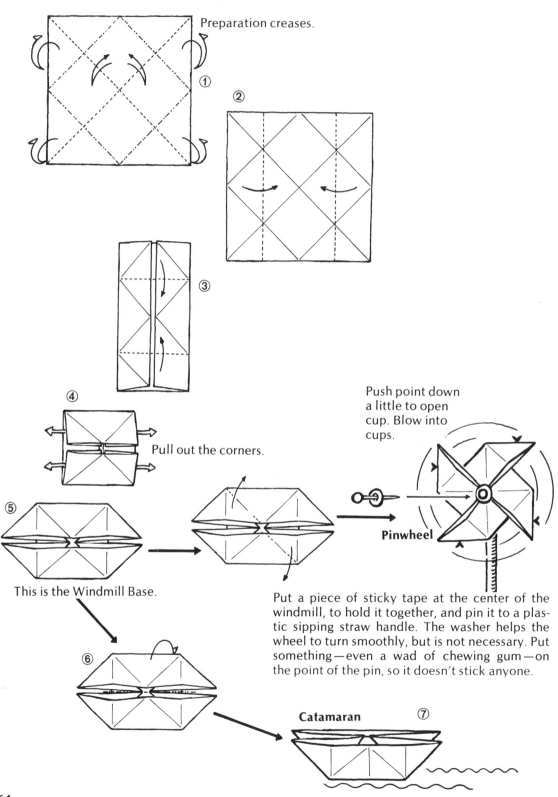

Preparation creases.

①

②

③

④ Pull out the corners.

⑤ This is the Windmill Base.

Push point down a little to open cup. Blow into cups.

Pinwheel

Put a piece of sticky tape at the center of the windmill, to hold it together, and pin it to a plastic sipping straw handle. The washer helps the wheel to turn smoothly, but is not necessary. Put something—even a wad of chewing gum—on the point of the pin, so it doesn't stick anyone.

⑥

Catamaran ⑦

Traditional

Begin with Windmill Base.

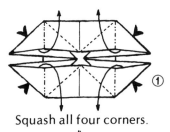

 ①

Squash all four corners.

These are preparation folds.

 ②

Take out preparation folds.

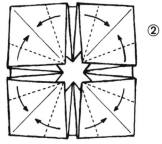 ③

Pull up one layer of paper and fold it back on the line shown. The edges will turn inward and meet at the center of the flap. This is a "Wing Fold."

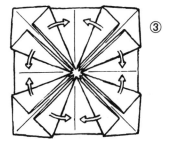 ④

 ⑥

Table

⑤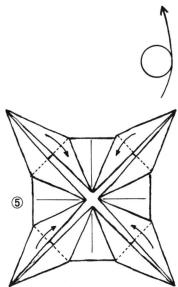

Fold up legs.

Two-piece Helicopter

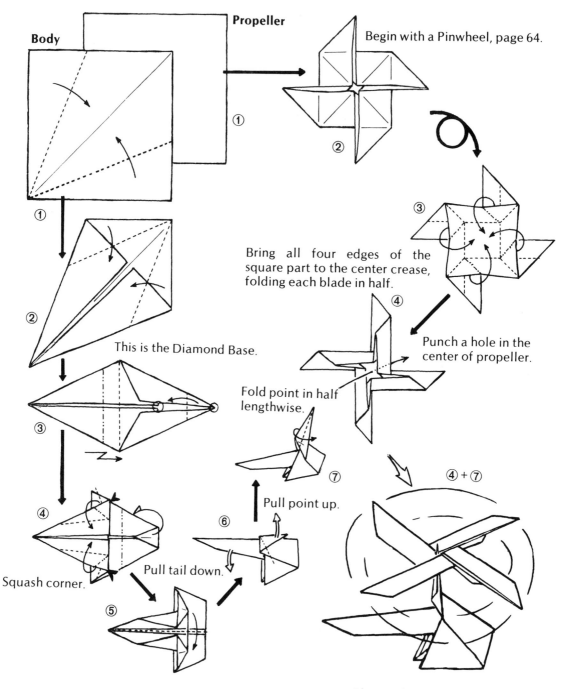

Propeller

Body

① Begin with a Pinwheel, page 64.

②

③ Bring all four edges of the square part to the center crease, folding each blade in half.

④ Punch a hole in the center of propeller.

②

This is the Diamond Base.

③

Fold point in half lengthwise.

⑦

④

Pull point up.

④ + ⑦

Squash corner.

⑥

Pull tail down.

⑤

Blow and propeller will turn.

66

by Kunihiko Kasahara

Two-piece Windmill

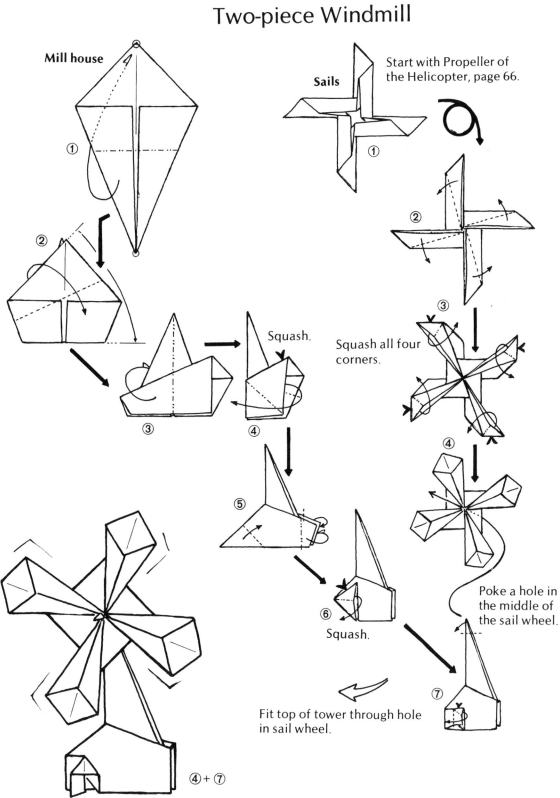

Mill house

①

②

③

④

Squash.

⑤

⑥

Squash.

Fit top of tower through hole
in sail wheel.

④ + ⑦

Sails

Start with Propeller of
the Helicopter, page 66.

①

②

③

Squash all four
corners.

④

Poke a hole in
the middle of
the sail wheel.

⑦

by Kunihiko Kasahara

Crown

You will need eleven pieces six inches square to make a child's crown. One for an adult takes twelve.

Fold all the pieces alike.

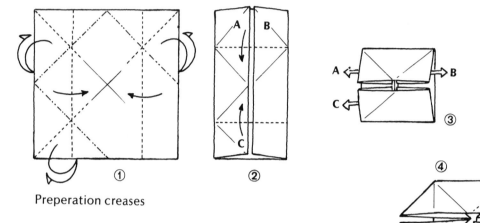

Preperation creases

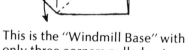

This is the "Windmill Base" with only three corners pulled out.

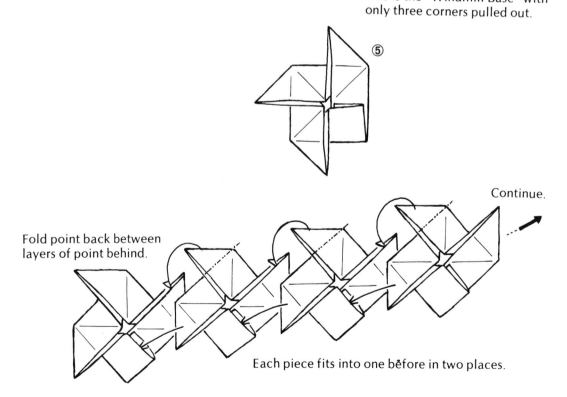

Fold point back between layers of point behind.

Each piece fits into one before in two places.

Continue.

by Kunihiko Kasahara

The Blintz Base

This base is named after a kind of pastry that has filling wrapped in a square of dough with the four corners meeting on top.

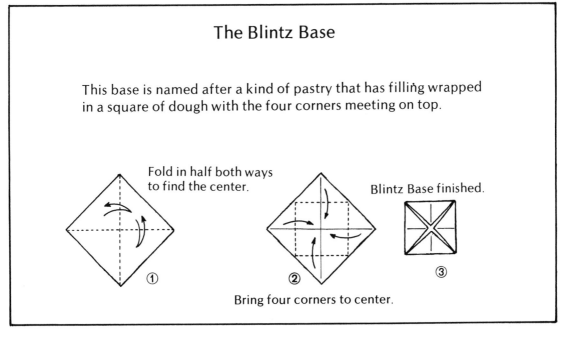

Fold in half both ways to find the center.

Blintz Base finished.

①   ②   ③

Bring four corners to center.

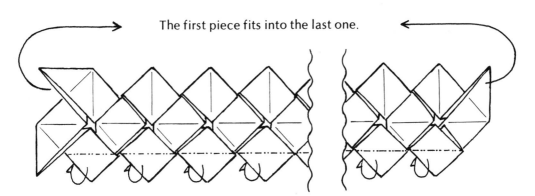

The first piece fits into the last one.

Turning the bottom corners back locks the pieces together. You don't have to glue them.

Camera

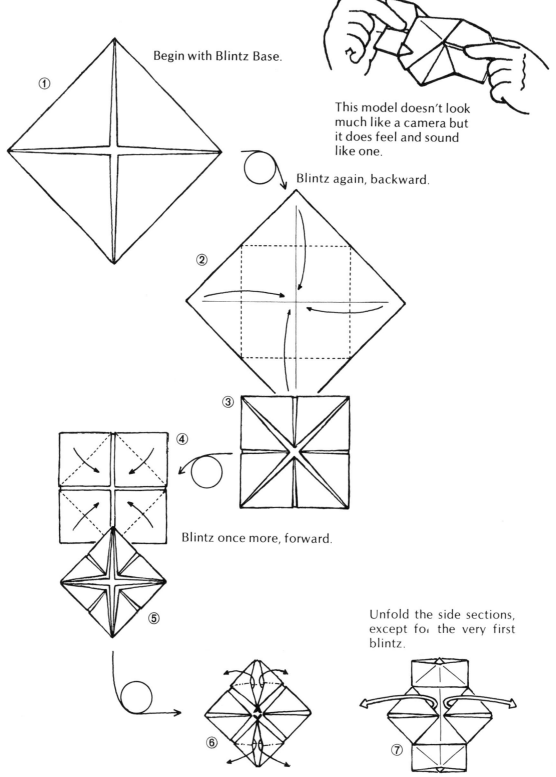

① Begin with Blintz Base.

This model doesn't look much like a camera but it does feel and sound like one.

Blintz again, backward.

②

③

④

Blintz once more, forward.

⑤

Unfold the side sections, except for the very first blintz.

⑥

⑦

Traditional — said to have been invented by children

Turn model over. Hold by the ends, with your thumbs at the center of the model.

⑬

Pull the ends back and push down on the center. The lock will pop open with a click.

⑭

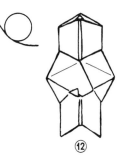

⑫

Refold the lock before making another "exposure".

Lock A and B together by folding tips over edges.

⑪

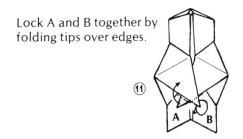

Cross A and B.

To do this, stand the flaps upright and pull them together.

⑩

A   B

Turn side sections inside out while folding model in half crosswise.

⑧

Fold back half down.

⑨

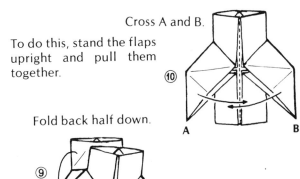

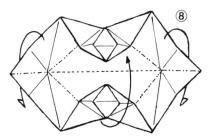

Basket

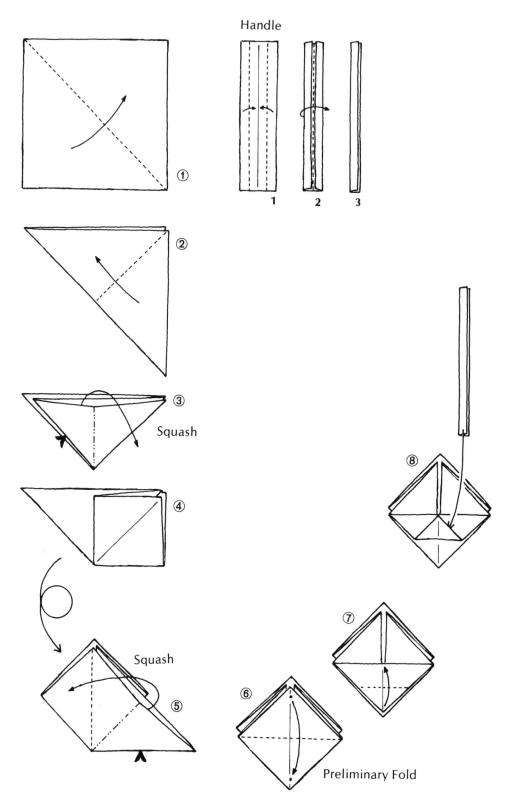

Handle

①

②

③ Squash

④

⑤ Squash

⑥

⑦

⑧

Preliminary Fold

1   2   3

by James M. Sakoda, U.S.A.

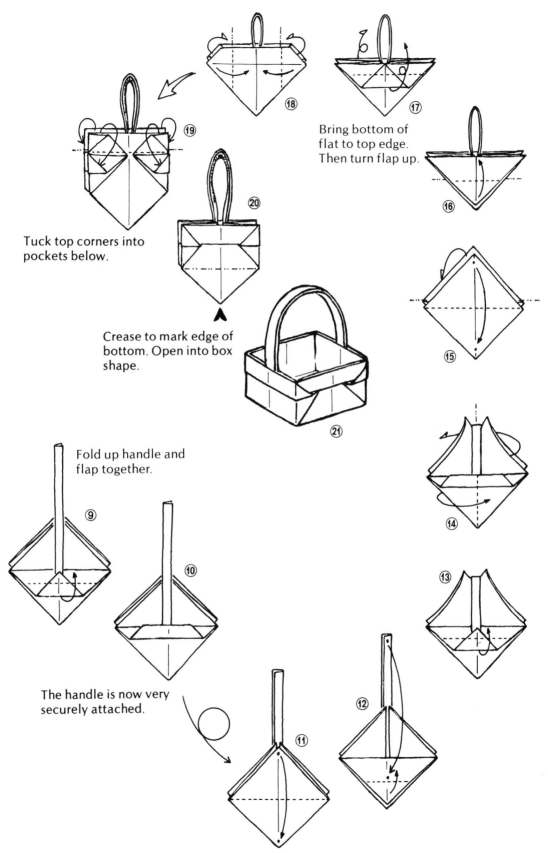

Bring bottom of
flat to top edge.
Then turn flap up.

Tuck top corners into
pockets below.

Crease to mark edge of
bottom. Open into box
shape.

Fold up handle and
flap together.

The handle is now very
securely attached.

⑱ ⑰ ⑯ ⑮ ⑭ ⑬ ⑲ ⑳ ㉑ ⑨ ⑩ ⑪ ⑫

Water-bomb Base and Balloon

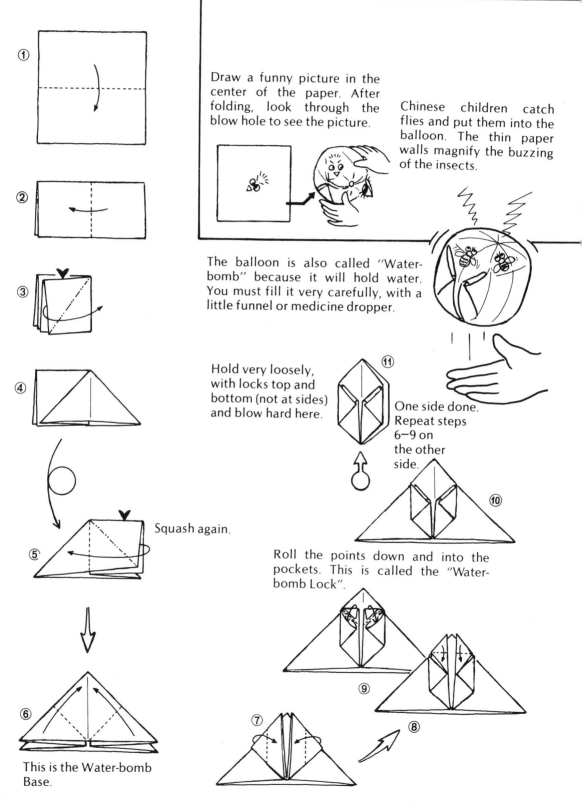

①

②

③

④

⑤ Squash again.

⑥ This is the Water-bomb Base.

⑦

⑧

⑨

⑩

⑪ One side done. Repeat steps 6–9 on the other side.

Draw a funny picture in the center of the paper. After folding, look through the blow hole to see the picture.

Chinese children catch flies and put them into the balloon. The thin paper walls magnify the buzzing of the insects.

The balloon is also called "Water-bomb" because it will hold water. You must fill it very carefully, with a little funnel or medicine dropper.

Hold very loosely, with locks top and bottom (not at sides) and blow hard here.

Roll the points down and into the pockets. This is called the "Water-bomb Lock".

Faceted Water-bomb

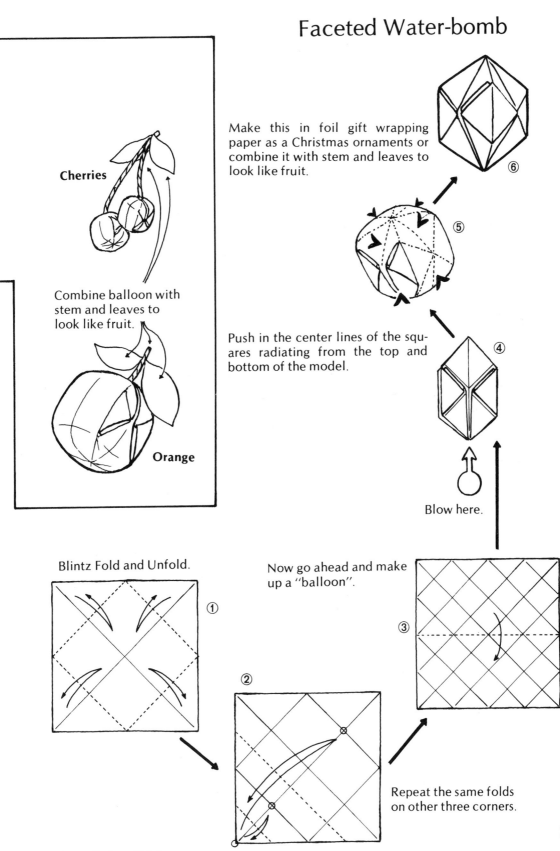

Cherries

Combine balloon with stem and leaves to look like fruit.

Orange

Make this in foil gift wrapping paper as a Christmas ornaments or combine it with stem and leaves to look like fruit.

⑥

⑤

Push in the center lines of the squares radiating from the top and bottom of the model.

④

Blow here.

Blintz Fold and Unfold.

Now go ahead and make up a "balloon".

①

②

③

Repeat the same folds on other three corners.

a variation by Endla Saar, U.S.A.

Boxers or Tulip Flower

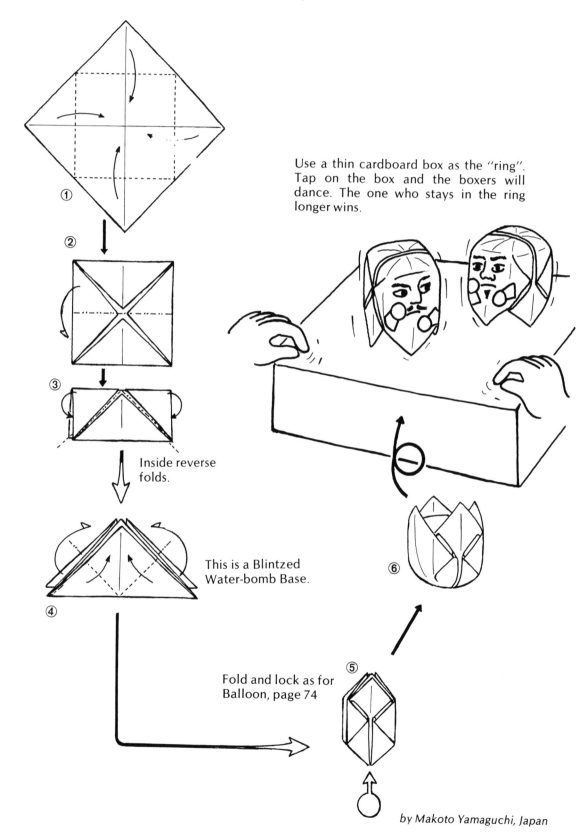

① ②

Use a thin cardboard box as the "ring". Tap on the box and the boxers will dance. The one who stays in the ring longer wins.

③

Inside reverse folds.

This is a Blintzed Water-bomb Base.

④

⑥

Fold and lock as for Balloon, page 74

⑤

by Makoto Yamaguchi, Japan

Stem and Leaf for Tulip

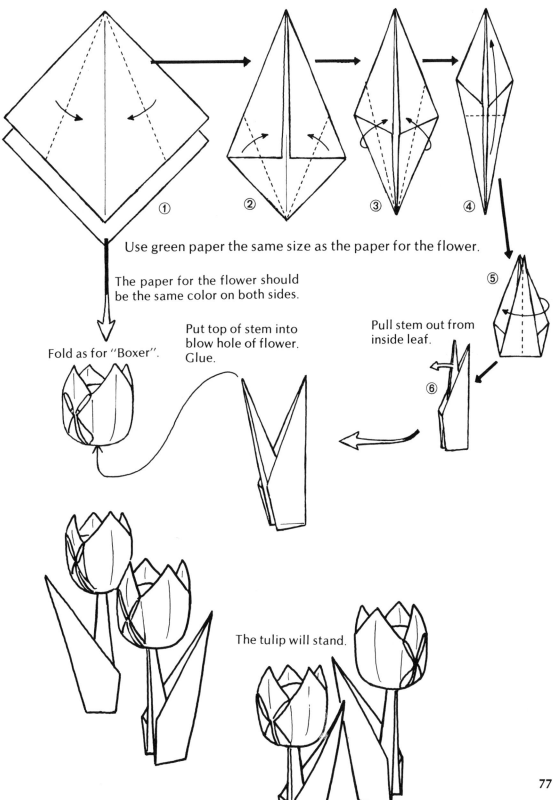

Use green paper the same size as the paper for the flower.

The paper for the flower should be the same color on both sides.

① ② ③ ④ ⑤ ⑥

Fold as for "Boxer".

Put top of stem into blow hole of flower. Glue.

Pull stem out from inside leaf.

The tulip will stand.

77

by Kunihiko Kasahara

Six Waterbomb Base Ornament

This model is made of six Water-bomb Bases, two of each of three colors.

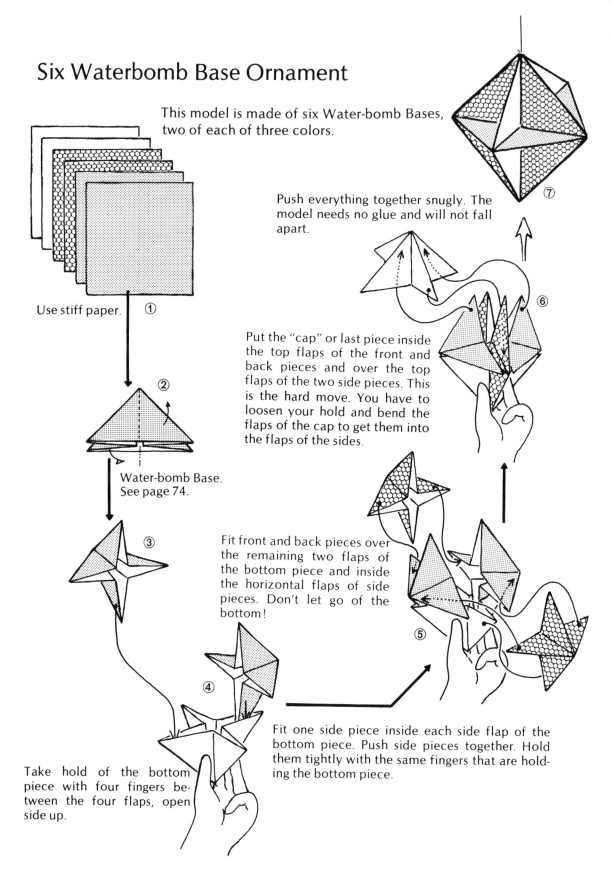

Use stiff paper. ①

Water-bomb Base.
See page 74.

②

③

④

Take hold of the bottom piece with four fingers between the four flaps, open side up.

Push everything together snugly. The model needs no glue and will not fall apart.

⑦

Put the "cap" or last piece inside the top flaps of the front and back pieces and over the top flaps of the two side pieces. This is the hard move. You have to loosen your hold and bend the flaps of the cap to get them into the flaps of the sides.

⑥

⑤

Fit front and back pieces over the remaining two flaps of the bottom piece and inside the horizontal flaps of side pieces. Don't let go of the bottom!

Fit one side piece inside each side flap of the bottom piece. Push side pieces together. Hold them tightly with the same fingers that are holding the bottom piece.

78

by Robert Neale, U.S.A.

How to Make an Origami Mobile

A mobile is a hanging ornament of many parts that move. Origami is good for mobile, because it weights so little. It moves easily and you can hang it from a support that is not very strong — a lamp fixture, for instance.
Fish, birds, boats, airplanes and other things that float or fly make the best mobiles.

To make a mobile, you will need, in addition to the origami models, a needle and some very strong thread, glue, some thin soft wire and a pair of wire cutters. If you prefer, you can use fine bamboo splints instead of wire.

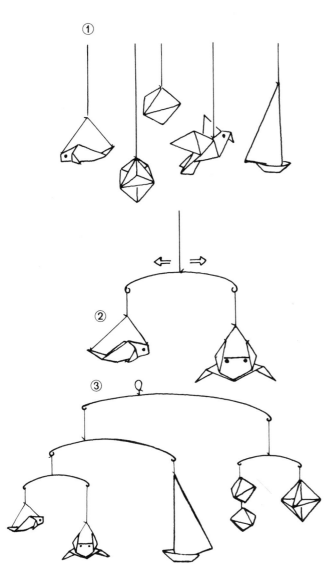

First, thread all your models, use as many threads as you need to make each one hang the way you want it.

Cut a piece of wire and tie a model to each end. A little loop at the end of the wire will keep the thread from slipping off. Glue the knots.

Tie a thread to the middle of the wire and slide it back and forth until the models balance. Then, glue the knot to the wire.

Tie the pair of models to one end of a longer wire. Put one model or another pair at the other end. Tie a thread to the wire and balance, as before.

Keep right on, working from the bottom upward and using longer and longer wires, until all your models have been hung. The wires must be long enough so that none of the models touch one another as they go around in circles. Hung up the mobile by the last balancing thread.

Fish Base and Fish

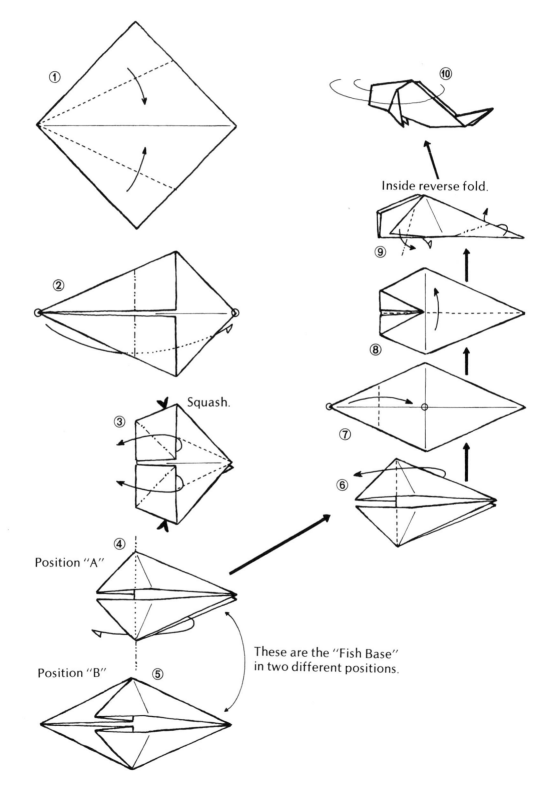

①

②

③ Squash.

④ Position "A"

⑤ Position "B"

These are the "Fish Base" in two different positions.

⑥

⑦

⑧

⑨ Inside reverse fold.

⑩

Traditional

Valentine Letterfold

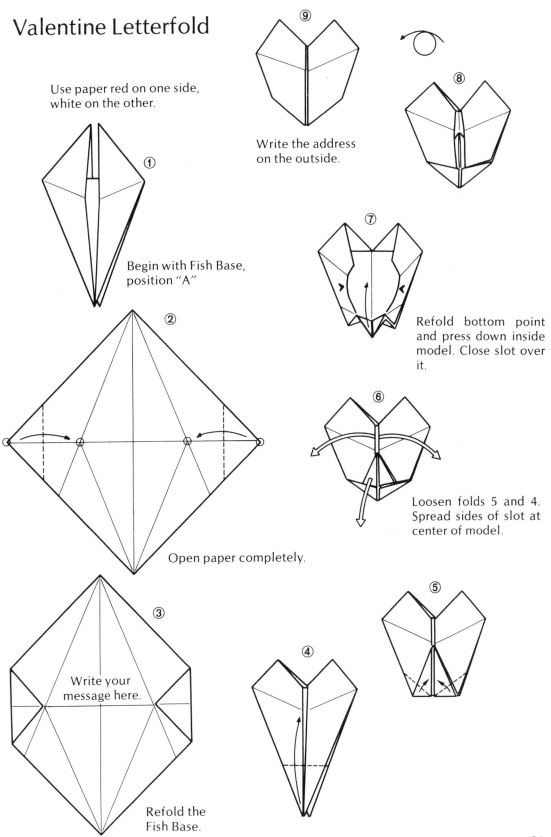

Use paper red on one side, white on the other.

① Begin with Fish Base, position "A"

② Open paper completely.

③ Write your message here.

Refold the Fish Base.

④

⑤

⑥ Loosen folds 5 and 4. Spread sides of slot at center of model.

⑦ Refold bottom point and press down inside model. Close slot over it.

⑧

⑨ Write the address on the outside.

by Alice Gray and Michael Shall

Two-piece Alligator

Begin with two squares alike, both folded into Fish Bases. (See page 80.)

Pull down inner layer.

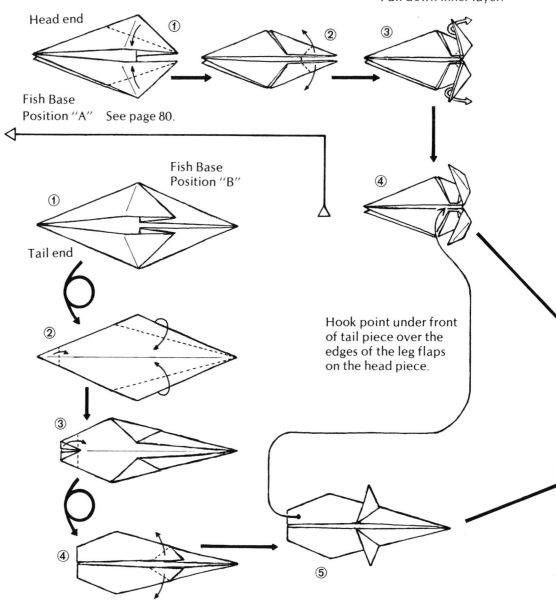

Head end

① ② ③

Fish Base
Position "A"   See page 80.

Fish Base
Position "B"

④

①

Tail end

②

③

Hook point under front of tail piece over the edges of the leg flaps on the head piece.

④

⑤

P 82   by Kunihiko Kasahara

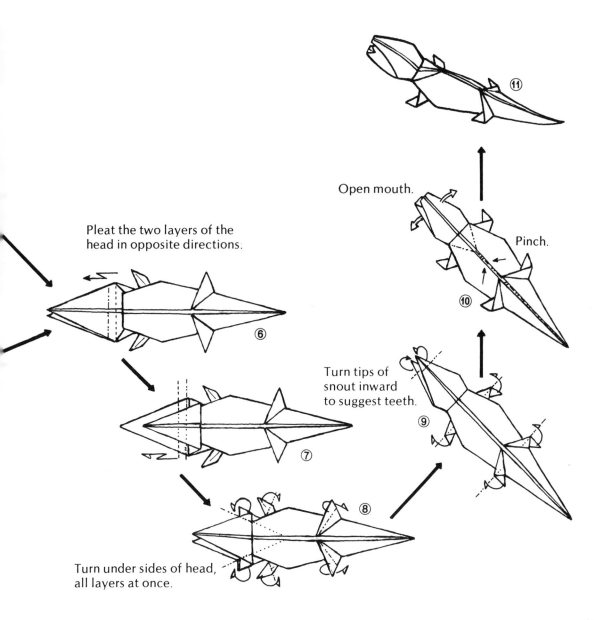

Pleat the two layers of the head in opposite directions.

⑥

Open mouth.

Pinch.

⑩

⑪

Turn tips of snout inward to suggest teeth.

⑨

⑦

⑧

Turn under sides of head, all layers at once.

Bird Base and Crane

The Bird Base is the most useful base in origami. It is used not only for birds but for hundreds of other models too.

The Crane (*Orizuru*) for which the base is named is the most famous of origami models. Nobody knows who created it, or when, but today thousands of people who know no other origami can make this.

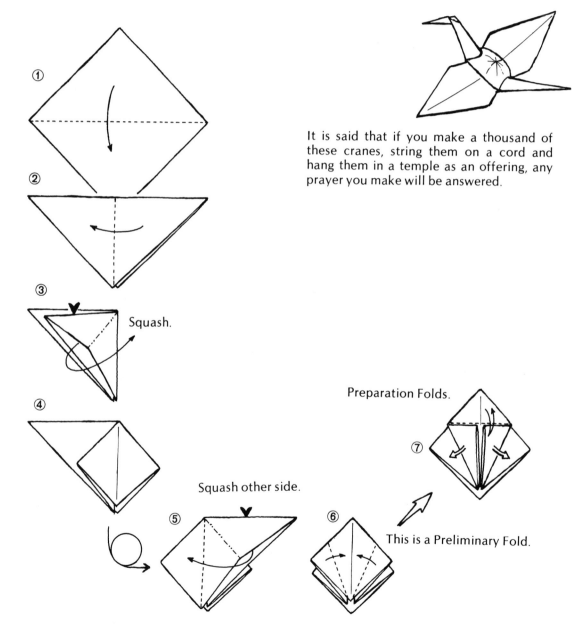

It is said that if you make a thousand of these cranes, string them on a cord and hang them in a temple as an offering, any prayer you make will be answered.

①

②

③ Squash.

④ Squash other side.

⑤

⑥ This is a Preliminary Fold.

⑦ Preparation Folds.

The famous "Lucky" Crane.

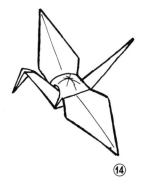

⑭

"Lover's knot Move". See page 31.

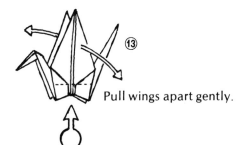

⑬

Pull wings apart gently.

Inflate the body by blowing into the hole in the bottom.

⑫

Inside reverse fold.

⑪

Inside reverse folds, as high up under the wings as you can make them.

⑩

Repeat steps 7—9 on the other side.

⑨

This is the "wing" for which the "Wing Fold" is named.

This is the completed Bird Base.

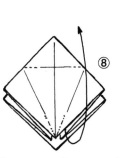

⑧

Lift upper layer only and press it down on crosswise crease. Edges roll inward and meet.

Flapping Bird and Flapping Crane

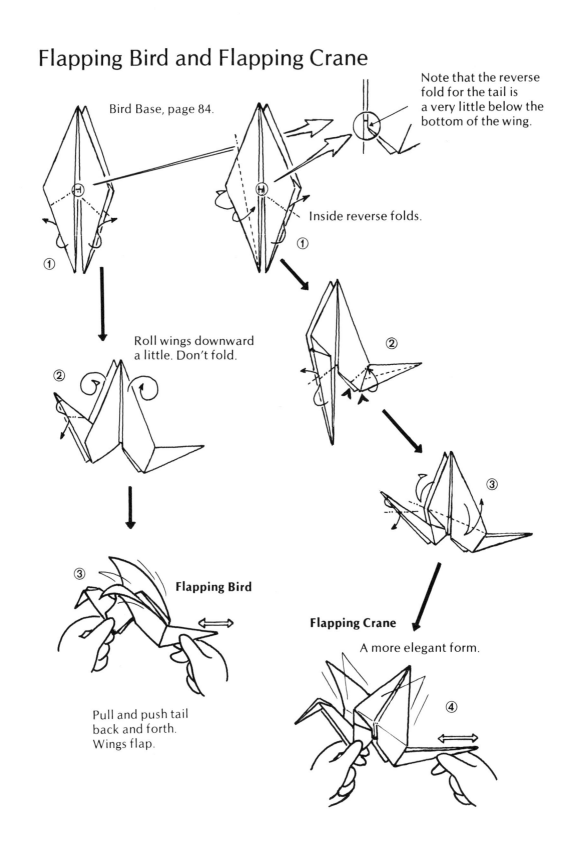

Bird Base, page 84.

Note that the reverse fold for the tail is a very little below the bottom of the wing.

Inside reverse folds.

①

①

Roll wings downward a little. Don't fold.

②

②

Flapping Bird

③

③

Pull and push tail back and forth. Wings flap.

Flapping Crane

A more elegant form.

④

Pop Star

Use two pieces of paper or foil, of strongly contrasting colors, the brighter on top. Put two sheets back to back and fold as one.

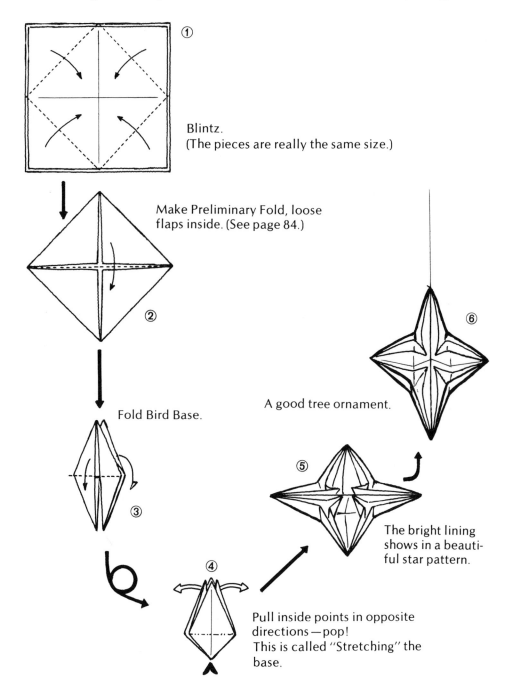

① Blintz.
(The pieces are really the same size.)

Make Preliminary Fold, loose flaps inside. (See page 84.)

②

Fold Bird Base.

③

④ Pull inside points in opposite directions—pop!
This is called "Stretching" the base.

⑤ The bright lining shows in a beautiful star pattern.

⑥ A good tree ornament.

Snail

Begin with Bird Base, page 84.

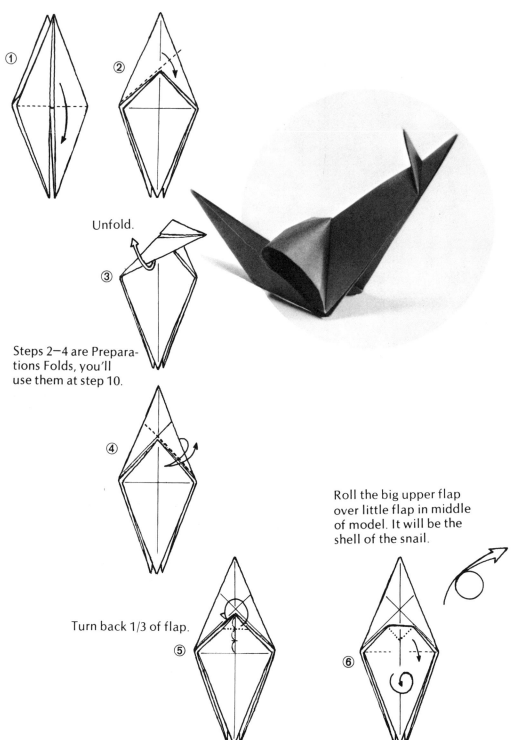

① ②

Unfold.

③

Steps 2–4 are Preparations Folds, you'll use them at step 10.

④

Roll the big upper flap over little flap in middle of model. It will be the shell of the snail.

Turn back 1/3 of flap.

⑤ ⑥

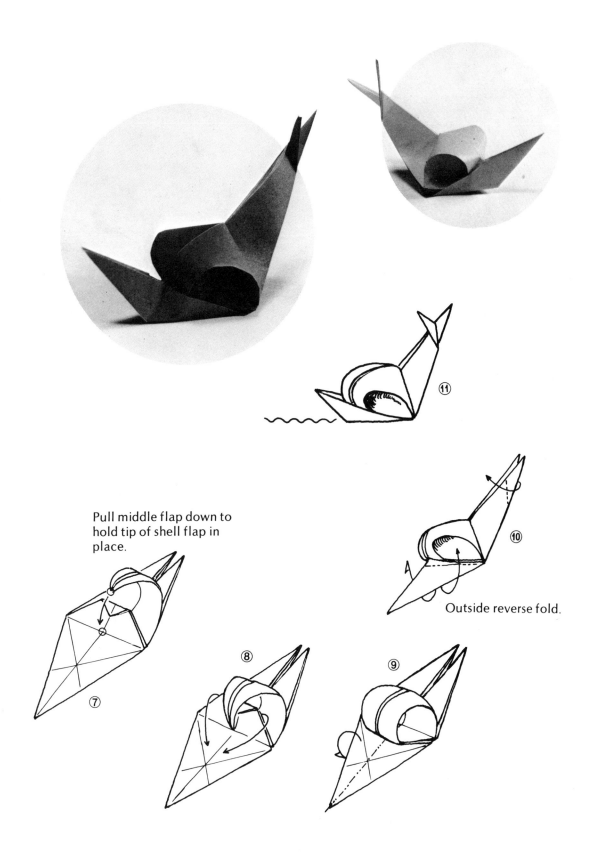

Pull middle flap down to
hold tip of shell flap in
place.

⑦

⑧

⑨

⑩

Outside reverse fold.

⑪

by Toshio Chino, Japan

Rabbit

Begin with Bird Base, page 84.

This is how the model looks from the edge.

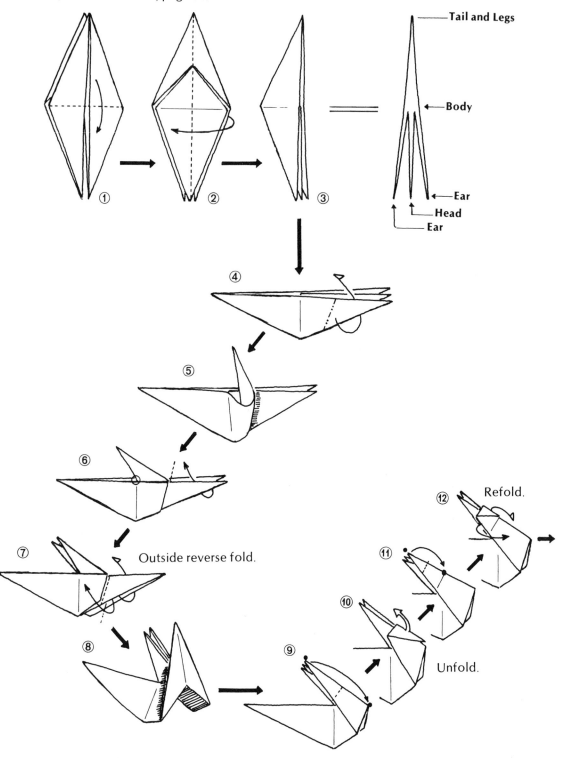

Tail and Legs

Body

Ear

Head

Ear

①   ②   ③   ④   ⑤   ⑥

⑦   Outside reverse fold.

⑧   ⑨   ⑩   ⑪   ⑫   Refold.

Unfold.

by Toshio Chino, Japan

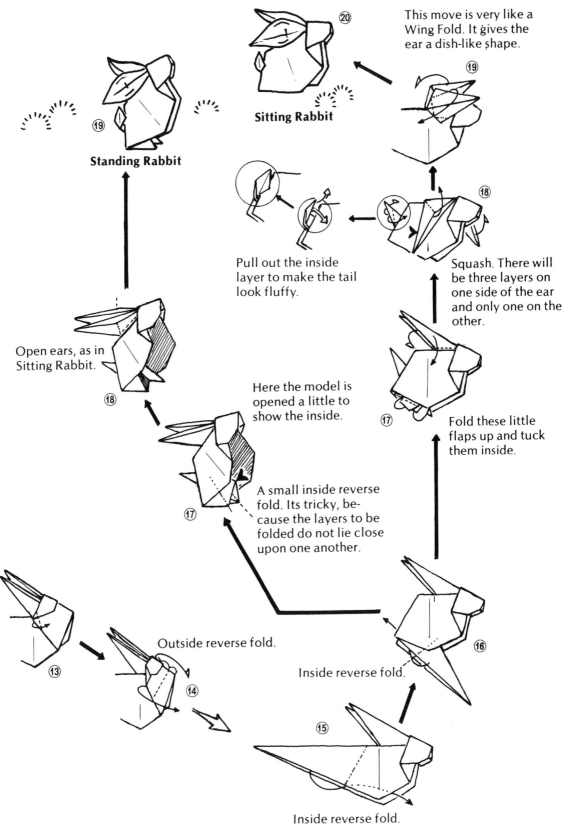

This move is very like a Wing Fold. It gives the ear a dish-like shape.

⑳

Sitting Rabbit

⑲

⑲

Standing Rabbit

⑱

Squash. There will be three layers on one side of the ear and only one on the other.

Pull out the inside layer to make the tail look fluffy.

Open ears, as in Sitting Rabbit.

⑱

Here the model is opened a little to show the inside.

⑰

Fold these little flaps up and tuck them inside.

⑰

A small inside reverse fold. Its tricky, because the layers to be folded do not lie close upon one another.

⑯

Outside reverse fold.

⑬

⑭

Inside reverse fold.

⑮

Inside reverse fold.

Frog or Lily Base

This is the most difficult to make of the traditional origami bases.
The frog made from it is a good one, but there are so many frogs
made from other bases that we prefer to call this the LILY BASE. We
don't know any other lily as good as the one made from this base.

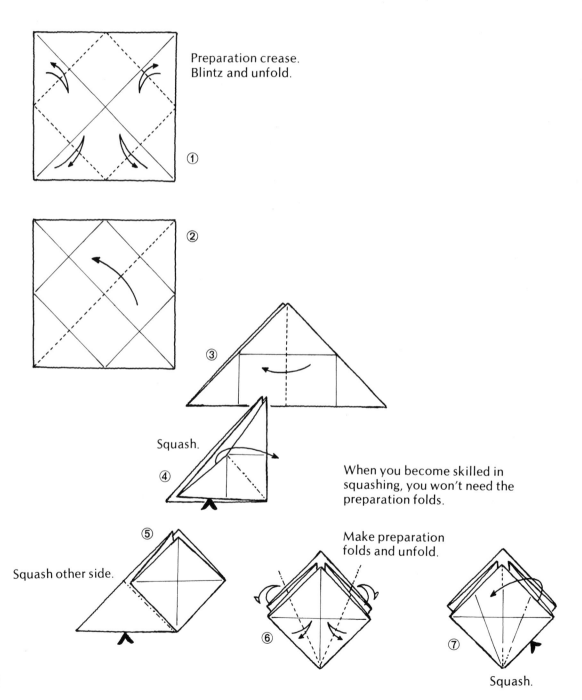

Preparation crease.
Blintz and unfold.

①

②

③

Squash.

④

When you become skilled in
squashing, you won't need the
preparation folds.

⑤

Squash other side.

Make preparation
folds and unfold.

⑥

⑦

Squash.

This is a "Petal Fold"

Repeat steps 13–15 on
other three sides.

⑮

Pull crosswise edge
down on line shown.
Edges turn in and meet.

⑭

Preparation crease,
fold and unfold.

⑬

Finished Frog or Lily Base.

Squash fourth flap.

⑫

Squash third flap.

⑪

Squash back flap.

⑧

⑨

⑩

Fold squashed
part in half
lengthwise. Re-
peat behind.

Turn over.

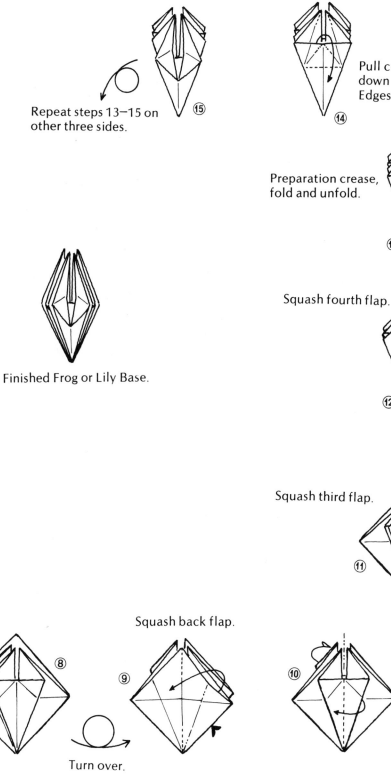

Lily and Iris

Begin with Lily Base, page 92.

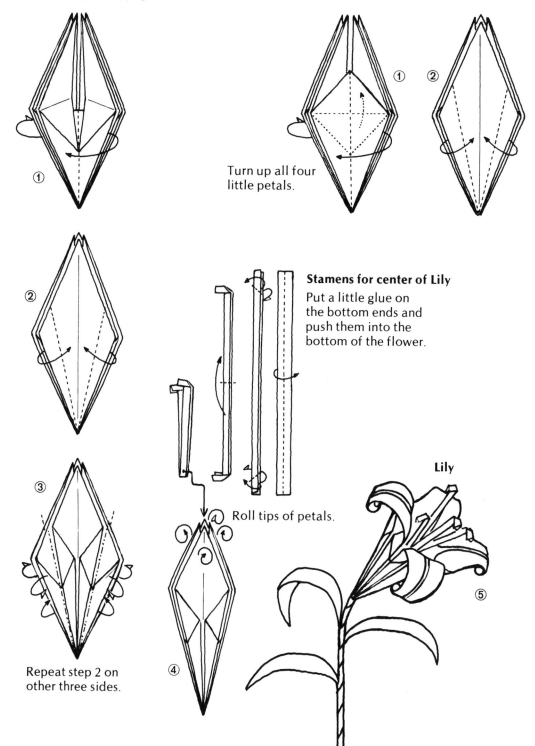

Turn up all four
little petals.

① ②

Repeat step 2 on
other three sides.

Stamens for center of Lily
Put a little glue on
the bottom ends and
push them into the
bottom of the flower.

Roll tips of petals.

Lily

Turn down all big petals.
You will have to loosen the
model a little to get at
the side ones.

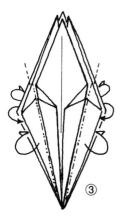

③

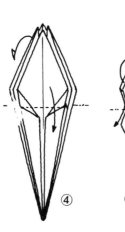

④

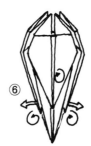

⑤

⑥

Repeat step 2 on
all other sides.

Open petals into horizontal
position and roll tips.

Iris

⑦

Lily Bud

Turn up all four
little petals.

①

②

Steps 2−3 turn in
edges of petals on
all four sides.

⑤

④

③

Roll tips
of petals.

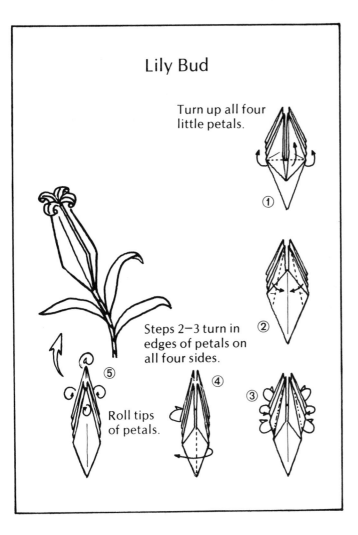

Jumping Frog

Begin with Frog or Lily Base, page 92.

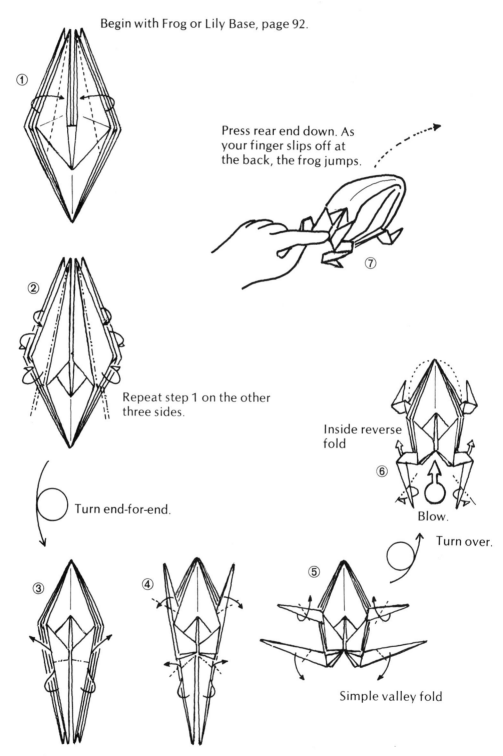

①

Press rear end down. As your finger slips off at the back, the frog jumps.

⑦

②

Repeat step 1 on the other three sides.

Inside reverse fold

⑥

Blow.

Turn end-for-end.

Turn over.

⑤

③

④

Simple valley fold

96 Inside reverse fold   Inside reverse fold

Traditional

Bell

Begin with the Frog or
Lily Base, page 92.

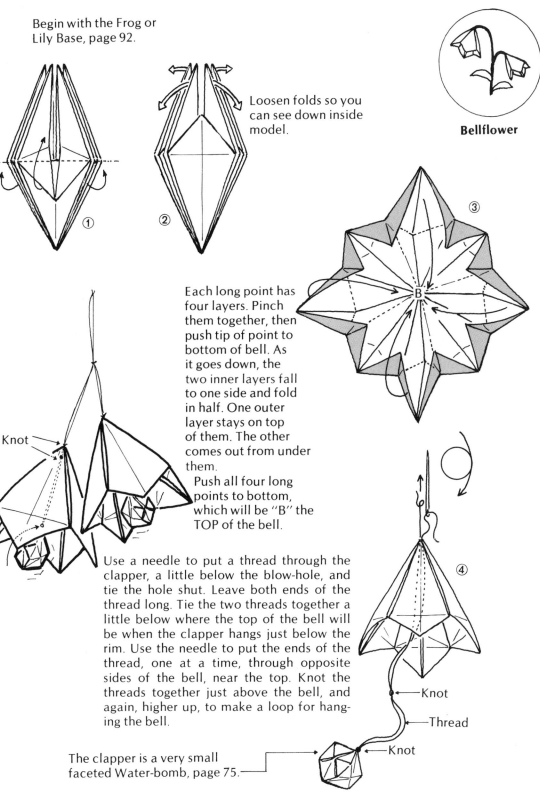

Loosen folds so you
can see down inside
model.

Bellflower

Each long point has
four layers. Pinch
them together, then
push tip of point to
bottom of bell. As
it goes down, the
two inner layers fall
to one side and fold
in half. One outer
layer stays on top
of them. The other
comes out from under
them.

Push all four long
points to bottom,
which will be "B" the
TOP of the bell.

Knot

Use a needle to put a thread through the
clapper, a little below the blow-hole, and
tie the hole shut. Leave both ends of the
thread long. Tie the two threads together a
little below where the top of the bell will
be when the clapper hangs just below the
rim. Use the needle to put the ends of the
thread, one at a time, through opposite
sides of the bell, near the top. Knot the
threads together just above the bell, and
again, higher up, to make a loop for hanging the bell.

The clapper is a very small
faceted Water-bomb, page 75.

Knot

Thread

Knot

an adaption of the traditional bell flower

Christmas Tree Ornaments

Any small, well-folded origami model can be a tree ornament, but those here are made only for Christmas trees. They are three-dimensional and geometric—thick as well as long and wide, and don't look like an anything in particular, just beautiful.

The ornaments look best when made of shiny metal foil gift-wrapping paper. Ask your friends to save you the wrapping from their gifts: that way you can get a lot of different colors and patterns in small quantities. If the paper is torn or wrinkled, cut off the damaged part. Hang up the ornaments with loops of thread, green or brown like the tree. Put the thread through the model at the end, not too close to the edge, with a needle.

The same model may look different, though equally good, when hung from the other end.

The whole family can help to decorate your tree. Some of the ornaments are easy enough for the very young, while others will challenge adult skill.

Not all the tree ornaments in this book are to be found in this section. There are others on pages 46, 47, 54, 56, 75, 78, 81, 87, 97, 117, 119, 120, 121, and 124.

How to Make a Square from an Irregular Piece of Paper

Because used gift wrappings are often without truly parallel sides, it may be difficult to get them square without measuring. A print trimmer makes the job easy. It cuts square corners automatically. All other ways of doing it depend on the same fact: if a straight line or edge is folded back upon itself, the new crease will be at right angles to the first line, that is, the corner formed by the two lines will be square. There are several ways of squaring by folding. Here is the one that gives the largest possible square with the fewest possible creases across it.

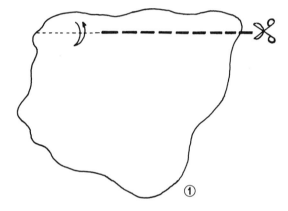

Make a fold as long as you can as close as you can come to the edge of the paper while leaving the damaged part outside. Cut on the fold.

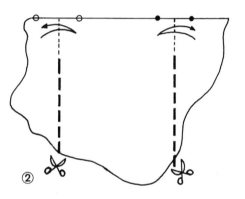

Make two creases that avoid damaged places. Imagine a square between them, and don't make them so far apart that the square would hang out at the bottom. Cut off sides.

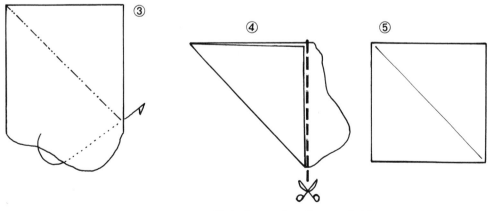

Cut along edge, then unfold.

Square Ornament with Shelves

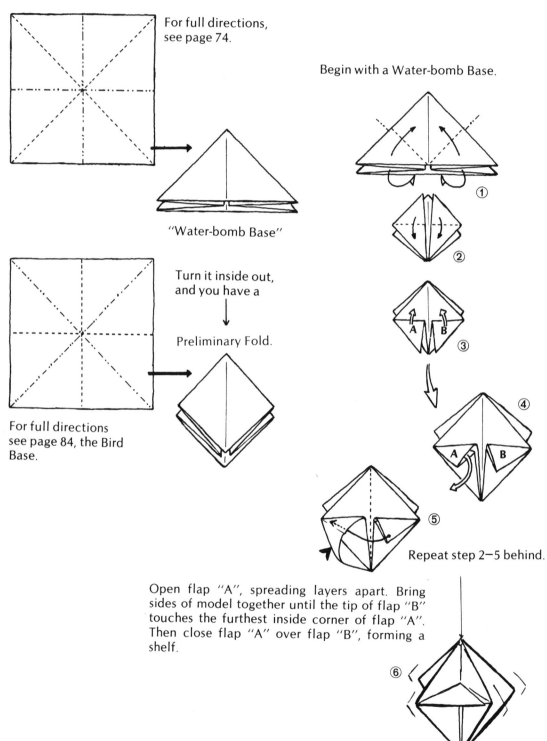

For full directions,
see page 74.

"Water-bomb Base"

Turn it inside out,
and you have a

Preliminary Fold.

For full directions
see page 84, the Bird
Base.

Begin with a Water-bomb Base.

① ② ③ ④ ⑤

Repeat step 2—5 behind.

Open flap "A", spreading layers apart. Bring
sides of model together until the tip of flap "B"
touches the furthest inside corner of flap "A".
Then close flap "A" over flap "B", forming a
shelf.

⑥

100

by Guiseppe Baggi, Italy

Diamond-shaped Ornament with Shelves

Begin with a Preliminary Fold.

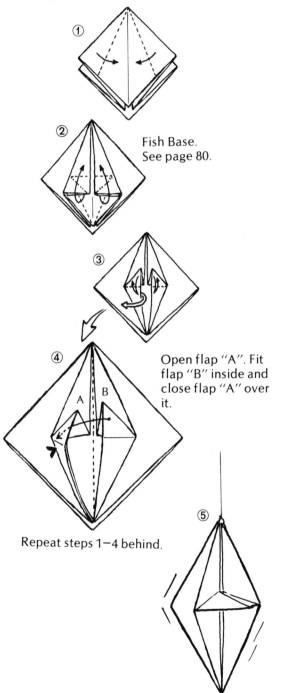

② Fish Base.
See page 80.

④ Open flap "A". Fit flap "B" inside and close flap "A" over it.

Repeat steps 1–4 behind.

by Guiseppe Baggi, Italy

Outside-inside Ornament

Use two pieces of paper of different colors front and back. Fold them alike and turn one inside-out. Of course, you can use any kind of paper, and just reverse the directions of the folds in one of them.

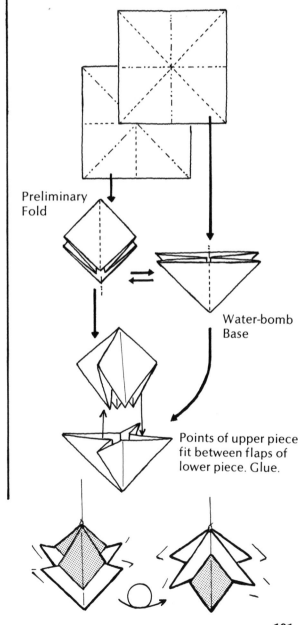

Preliminary Fold

Water-bomb Base

Points of upper piece fit between flaps of lower piece. Glue.

101

by Molly Kahn, U.S.A.

Crystal Tree Ornament

Use two rectangles. They can be halves of a square, but anything longer than square will work. The pieces may be of different colors. Fold both pieces in the same way.

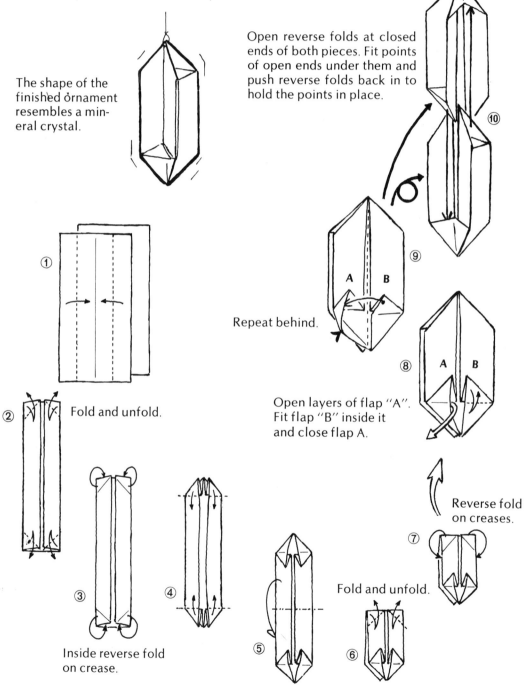

The shape of the finished ornament resembles a mineral crystal.

Open reverse folds at closed ends of both pieces. Fit points of open ends under them and push reverse folds back in to hold the points in place.

⑩

⑨

Repeat behind.

A   B

Open layers of flap "A". Fit flap "B" inside it and close flap A.

⑧   A   B

Reverse fold on creases.

⑦

Fold and unfold.

①

② Fold and unfold.

③ Inside reverse fold on crease.

④

⑤

⑥

by John M. Nordquist, U.S.A.

Eight Vaned Tree Ornament

Begin with Preliminary Fold, page 84. Make two pieces alike.

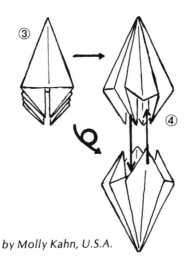

Squash.

Squash other three flaps.

by Molly Kahn, U.S.A.

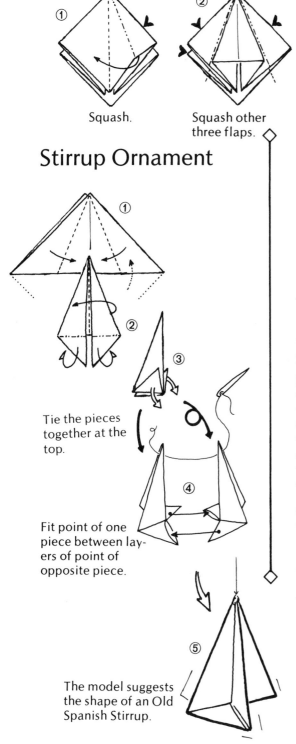

Stirrup Ornament

Tie the pieces together at the top.

Fit point of one piece between layers of point of opposite piece.

The model suggests the shape of an Old Spanish Stirrup.

To Assemble Eight Vaned Tree Ornament

Each piece has eight faces, alternately triangular and kite shaped, all folded in half lengthwise. The square point of each kite goes under the base of the opposite triangle, and the section is then valley folded in half on the crease already there. First, fit together one pair, then the next. Grasp the vane or mountain-folded flap that forms between the two sections as they are folded lengthwise with valley folds. Don't let go. Fit together a third section and valley fold the vane down on top of the first. Keep hold of both and proceed, the stacking the vanes and holding tight to the stack, until you come to the last section. Here you will have to bend the point to get it under the opposite edge. Push the ends of the model together snugly and arrange the eight vanes evenly. The more each end of the ornament tends to spring open, the more tightly it will clutch its partner. No glue is needed.

103

by Molly Kahn, U.S.A.

Drop-shaped Ornament

Strawberry Ornament

Begin with a Preliminary Fold, page 84.

I stumbled upon this one while trying to remember a strawberry with a burr on top invents by my friend, Mrs. Cooker.

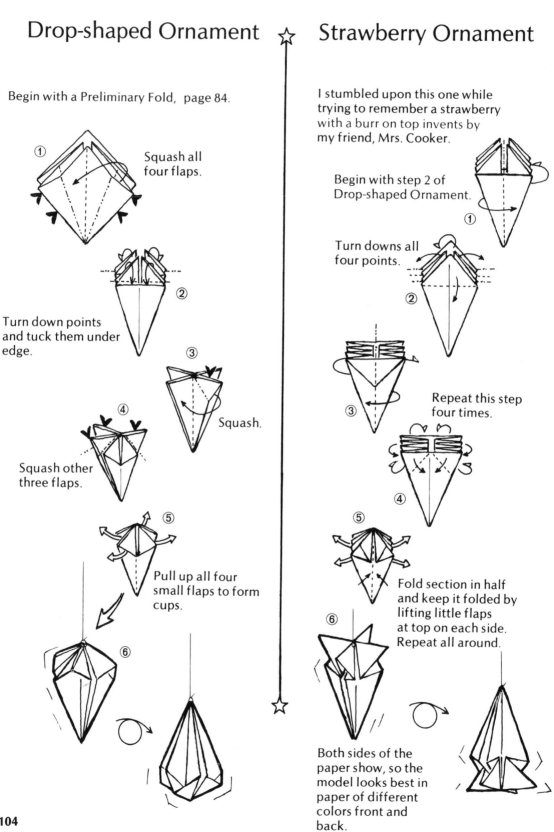

Squash all four flaps.

Turn down points and tuck them under edge.

Squash other three flaps.

Squash.

Pull up all four small flaps to form cups.

Begin with step 2 of Drop-shaped Ornament.

Turn downs all four points.

Repeat this step four times.

Fold section in half and keep it folded by lifting little flaps at top on each side. Repeat all around.

Both sides of the paper show, so the model looks best in paper of different colors front and back.

104

by Rae Cooker, U.S.A.

by Alice Gray

Lemon-shaped Ornament

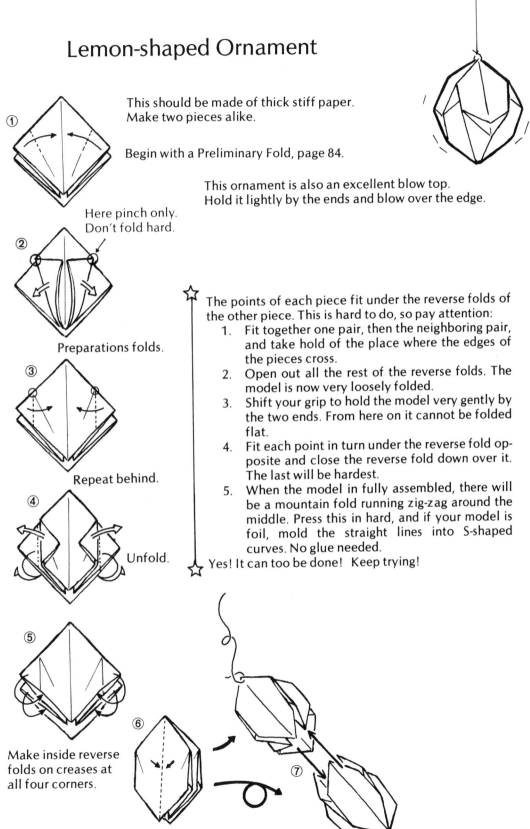

① This should be made of thick stiff paper.
Make two pieces alike.

Begin with a Preliminary Fold, page 84.

This ornament is also an excellent blow top.
Hold it lightly by the ends and blow over the edge.

Here pinch only.
Don't fold hard.

② Preparations folds.

③ Repeat behind.

④ Unfold.

⑤ Make inside reverse folds on creases at all four corners.

⑥

⑦

☆ The points of each piece fit under the reverse folds of the other piece. This is hard to do, so pay attention:

1. Fit together one pair, then the neighboring pair, and take hold of the place where the edges of the pieces cross.
2. Open out all the rest of the reverse folds. The model is now very loosely folded.
3. Shift your grip to hold the model very gently by the two ends. From here on it cannot be folded flat.
4. Fit each point in turn under the reverse fold opposite and close the reverse fold down over it. The last will be hardest.
5. When the model in fully assembled, there will be a mountain fold running zig-zag around the middle. Press this in hard, and if your model is foil, mold the straight lines into S-shaped curves. No glue needed.

☆ Yes! It can too be done! Keep trying!

105

by Alice Gray

Zig-zag Tree Ornament

So called because of the pattern formed
by the reverse folds around the middle.

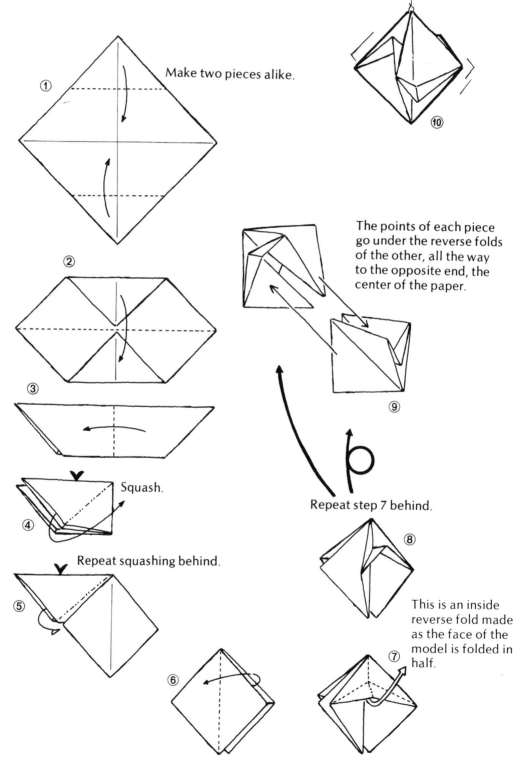

Make two pieces alike.

The points of each piece
go under the reverse folds
of the other, all the way
to the opposite end, the
center of the paper.

Repeat step 7 behind.

Squash.

Repeat squashing behind.

This is an inside
reverse fold made
as the face of the
model is folded in
half.

by Alice Gray

Octahedron

This model was independently invented by at least two people, Robert Neale and Rae Cooker, both, U.S.A.

Make two pieces alike. Use stiff paper of different color on the two sides. If both pieces are started with the same side up, the model will be checkered. If one piece is up-side-down, the model will be striped.

Begin with a Preliminary Fold, page 84.

①

If, at step 1 the points are folded inward instead of outward, the model will be the same color allover.

②

Squash.

Squashs other three flaps.

③

④

The little flaps being formed here must, at step 7, stand at right angles to the main flap, to which they are attached. Otherwise the model comes apart.

⑧

No glue needed.

The point of each diamond goes under the edge of the opposite triangle.

⑦

Pinch. — Pinch.

⑥

⑤

Embroidered Ball

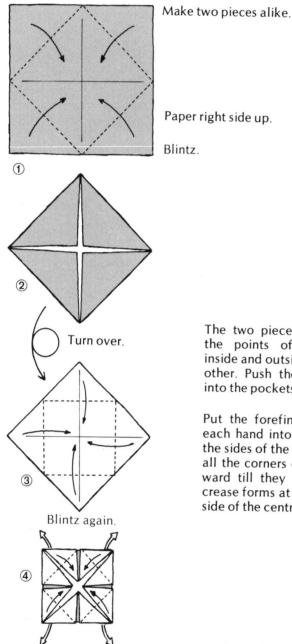

Make two pieces alike.

Paper right side up.

Blintz.

①

②

Turn over.

③

Blintz again.

④

Blintz a third time, letting the points up from below. This brings the right side of the paper out, on the under side.

The two pieces go together with the points of each alternately inside and outside the points of the other. Push the points as far up into the pockets as they will go.

Put the forefinger and thumb of each hand into the pockets under the sides of the central square. Pull all the corners of the paper down-ward till they meet. A mountain crease forms at the middle of each side of the central square.

⑥

Turn tips.

Turn over.

⑤

Preparation folds. Put them in and take them out.

⑦

⑧

by Jack Skillman, U.S.A.

Ornamental Ball

Miss Gurkewitz was trying to remember the "Embroidered Ball" when she invented this one.

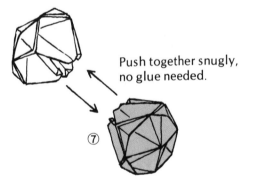

⑧

Make two pieces alike.

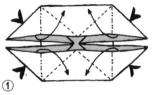

Begin with Windmill Base, page 64.

①

Squash all four points.

②

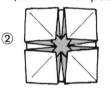

The points of each piece go alternately inside and outside the points of the other just as in the "Embroidered Ball".

Push together snugly, no glue needed.

⑦

Turn over.

③ Blintz, letting corners come up from underneath.

④

Turn over.

⑤

Blunt tips.

⑥

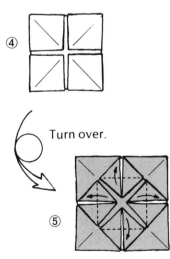

Pull the corners of the paper together downward and push the sides of the inner square upward, as in the "Embroidered Ball". Then open the little cups in the corners of the inner square by pulling up the edges.

109

by Rona Gurkewitz, U.S.A.

Christmas Tree

Use as many pieces as you like, each smaller than the one before by about 1/8 of the biggest square.

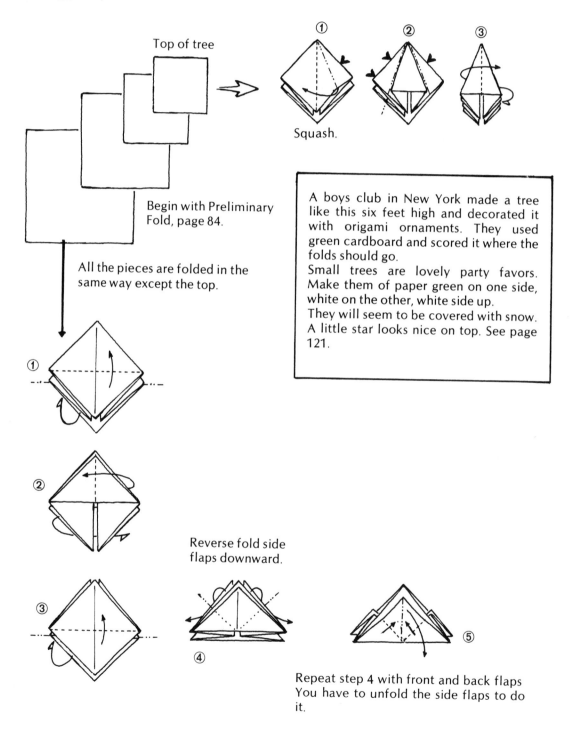

Top of tree

Squash.

Begin with Preliminary Fold, page 84.

A boys club in New York made a tree like this six feet high and decorated it with origami ornaments. They used green cardboard and scored it where the folds should go.
Small trees are lovely party favors. Make them of paper green on one side, white on the other, white side up.
They will seem to be covered with snow. A little star looks nice on top. See page 121.

All the pieces are folded in the same way except the top.

Reverse fold side flaps downward.

Repeat step 4 with front and back flaps You have to unfold the side flaps to do it.

Glue neighboring flaps together in four places, leaving four kite-shapes areas free.

Make the tree of thin paper. Fold it in half lengthwise and glue the fold into the fold of a greeting card. As the card opens, so does the tree.

Stack the pieces from the bottom up, not too closely, fastening each to the one below with glue. Push everything tightly together at the center of the model while the glue sets.

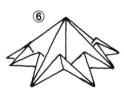

You now have a wheel of eight points.

by Rae Cooker, U.S.A.

Christmas Tree

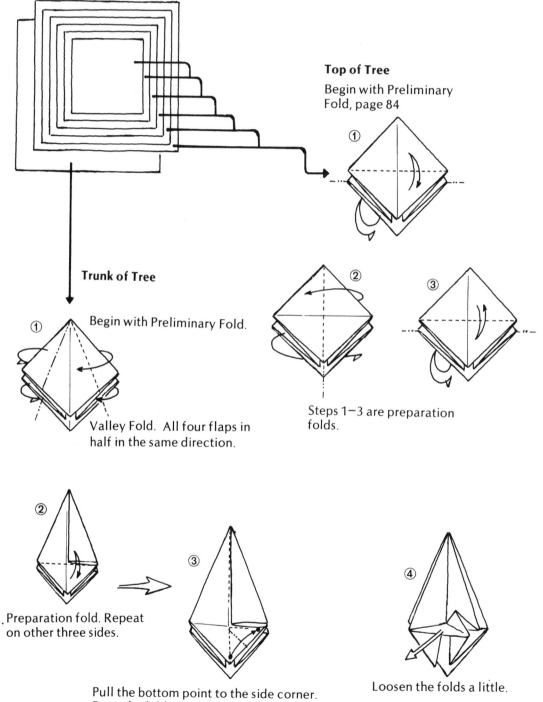

Top of Tree

Begin with Preliminary Fold, page 84

①

Trunk of Tree

① Begin with Preliminary Fold.

Valley Fold. All four flaps in half in the same direction.

②

③

Steps 1–3 are preparation folds.

② Preparation fold. Repeat on other three sides.

③ Pull the bottom point to the side corner. Press the folds to make them sharp.

④ Loosen the folds a little.

Independently invented by Rae Cooker, U.S.A. and Makoto Yamaguchi, Japan.

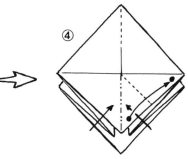

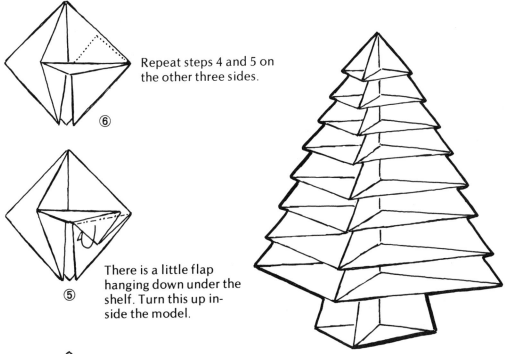

Repeat steps 4 and 5 on the other three sides.

⑥

There is a little flap hanging down under the shelf. Turn this up inside the model.

⑤

④ Pinch up the bottom half of the center crease into a mountain fold. Swing it over to lie along the right half of the horizontal crease. This pulls up the left flap and makes a shelf of the bottom half of it.

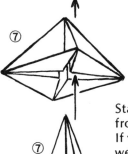

⑦

Stack the pieces from the trunk up. If you have folded well, they will fit snugly, but use a little glue if you wish.

⑤

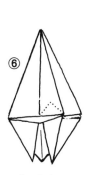

⑥

⑦

Tuck the little flap on the side of the shelf between the layers of the flap above it.

Finished shelf. Now repeat steps 2–5 on the other three sides.

Models Made from Paper of Other Shapes

Not Rectangular or Square

Such models are unusual: there are not many of them but they are beautiful. The hardest part of making them is shaping the paper to begin with. Do it carefully, so the shape will be "true" and the models tidy.

How to Make an Isosceles Right Triangle from a Square

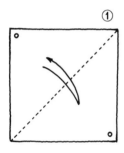

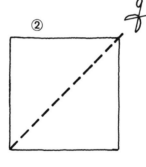

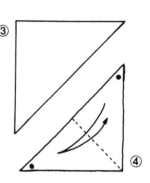

An Isosceles Triangle has two sides the same length.
A Right Triangle has one corner square.

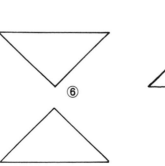

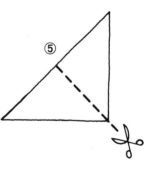

Mouse

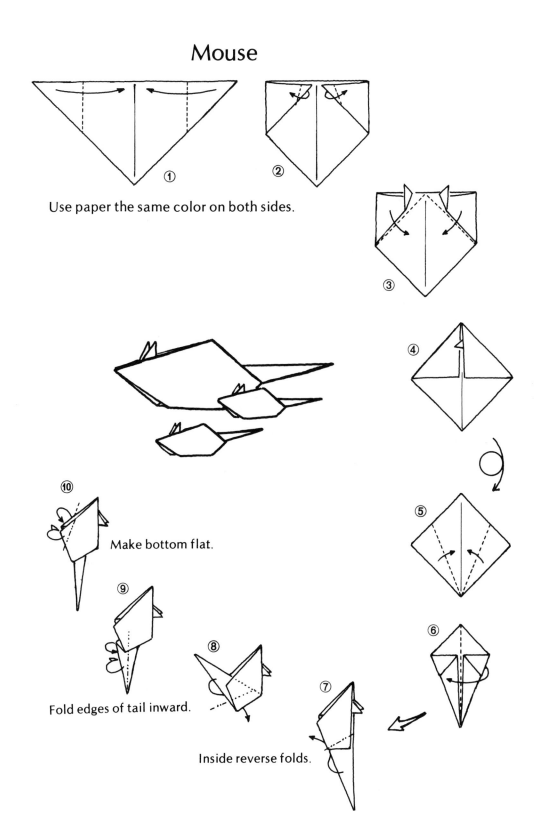

Use paper the same color on both sides.

Make bottom flat.

Fold edges of tail inward.

Inside reverse folds.

115

by Kunihiko Kasahara

How to Make an Equilateral Triangle from a Long Rectangle or Strip

An Equilateral Triangle has three sides the same length.

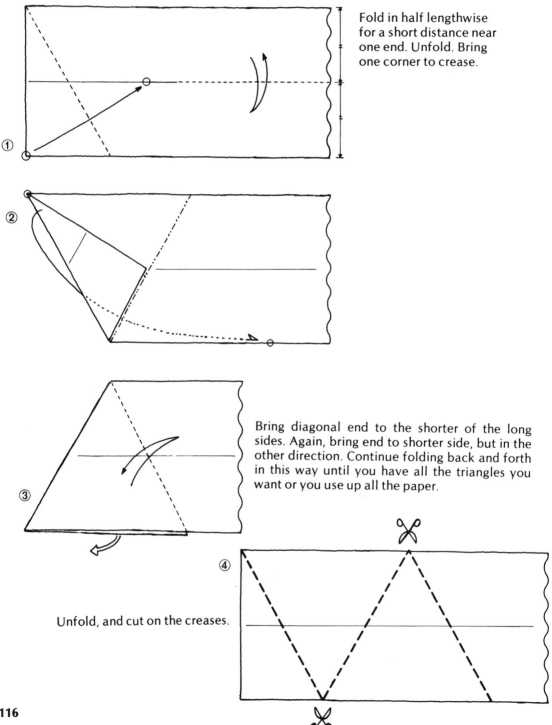

Fold in half lengthwise for a short distance near one end. Unfold. Bring one corner to crease.

Bring diagonal end to the shorter of the long sides. Again, bring end to shorter side, but in the other direction. Continue folding back and forth in this way until you have all the triangles you want or you use up all the paper.

Unfold, and cut on the creases.

Star of David

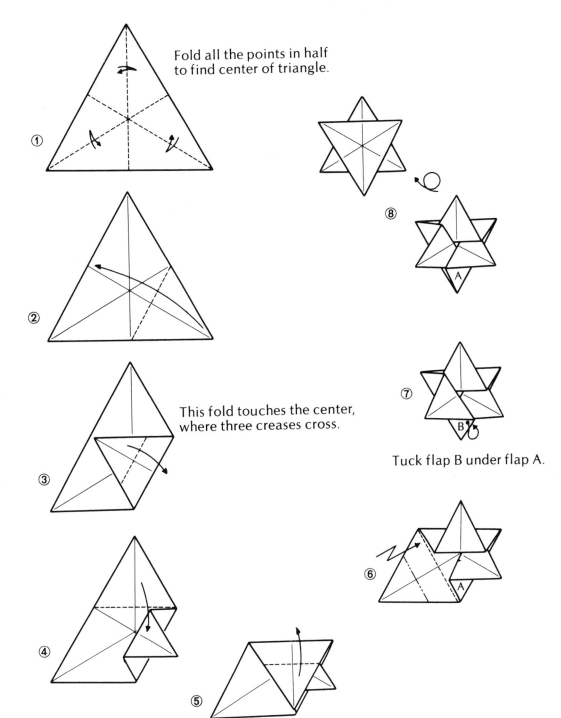

Fold all the points in half to find center of triangle.

This fold touches the center, where three creases cross.

Tuck flap B under flap A.

by Lewis Simon, U.S.A.

How to Make a Regular Hexagon from a Long Rectangle or Strip

A Regular Hexagon has six sides the same length.

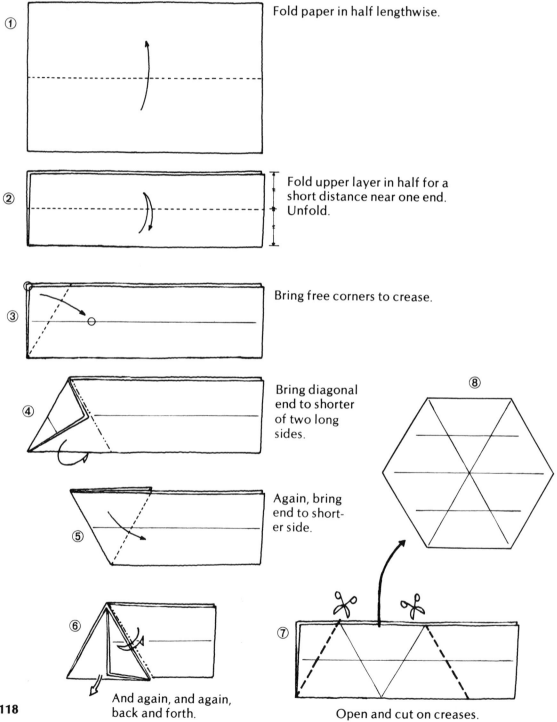

① Fold paper in half lengthwise.

② Fold upper layer in half for a short distance near one end. Unfold.

③ Bring free corners to crease.

④ Bring diagonal end to shorter of two long sides.

⑤ Again, bring end to shorter side.

⑥ And again, and again, back and forth.

⑦ Open and cut on creases.

⑧

Octahedron (eight sided solid)

Independently invented by Ryutaro Tsuchida, Kouji Fushimi with his wife Mitsue Fushimi, Japan and Patricia Crawford, U.S.A.

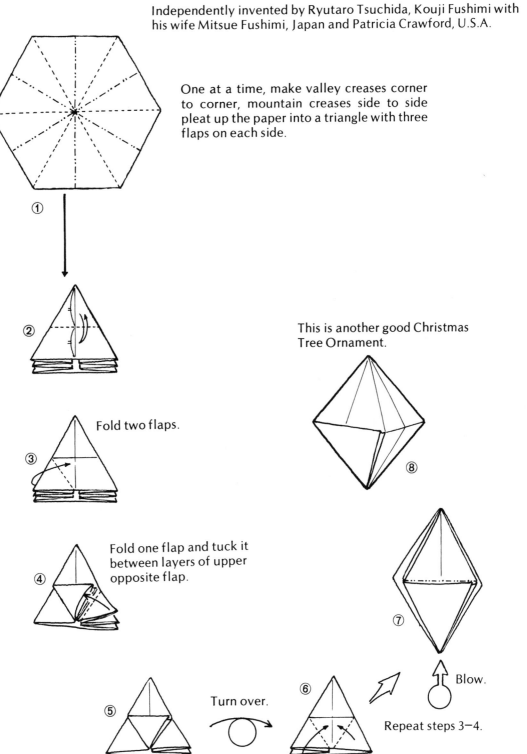

①

One at a time, make valley creases corner to corner, mountain creases side to side pleat up the paper into a triangle with three flaps on each side.

②

③ Fold two flaps.

④ Fold one flap and tuck it between layers of upper opposite flap.

⑤

Turn over.

⑥

Repeat steps 3—4.

Blow.

⑦

This is another good Christmas Tree Ornament.

⑧

How to Make a Regular Pentagon and Five-pointed Star from a Square

A Regular Pentagon has five sides, all the same length.

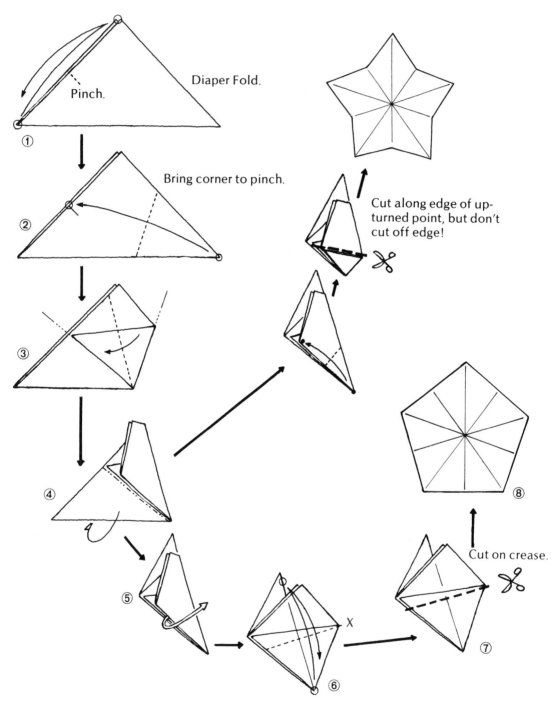

Diaper Fold.

Pinch.

①

② Bring corner to pinch.

③

④

⑤

⑥

X

Cut along edge of up-turned point, but don't cut off edge!

Cut on crease.

⑦

⑧

Crease must pass through point "X".

Star

Preparation creases:
Mountain folds from corners
to center, valley folds from
sides to center.

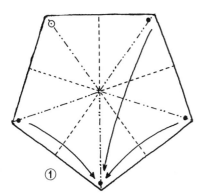

① Pleat up into broad kite shape.

②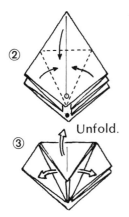

Unfold.

③

④ Wing fold.
(See Bird Base, page 84.)

Wing fold other four flaps.

⑤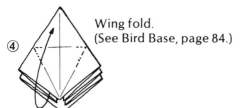

Make preparation fold,
then sink the top.

⑥

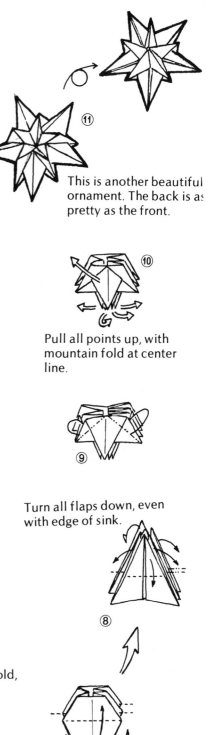

⑪

This is another beautiful
ornament. The back is as
pretty as the front.

⑩ Pull all points up, with
mountain fold at center
line.

⑨

Turn all flaps down, even
with edge of sink.

⑧

⑦ Pull all five wings up.

121

by Endla Saar, U.S.A.

How to Make a Regular Octagon from a Square

A regular octagon has eight sides, all the same length.

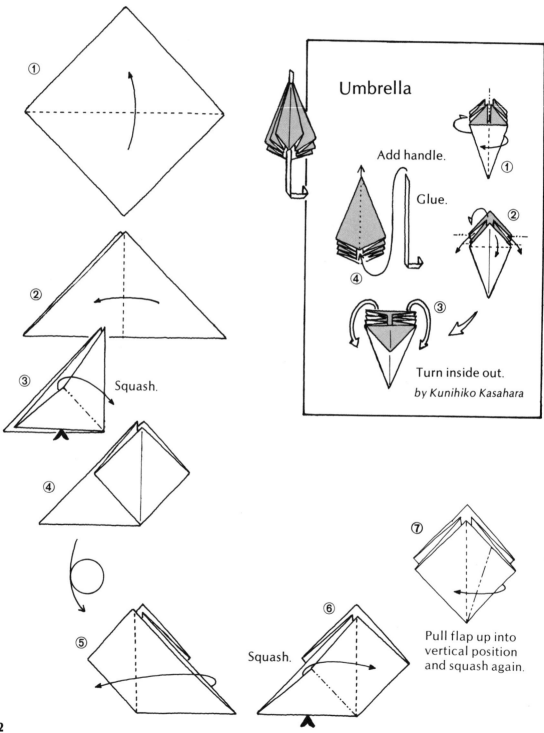

①

②

③ Squash.

④

⑤

Squash. ⑥

⑦

Pull flap up into vertical position and squash again.

Umbrella

①

②

③

④ Add handle. Glue.

Turn inside out.

by Kunihiko Kasahara

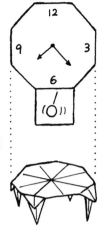

The Clock, page 63, and the
Table, page 65, are octagonal
when finished.

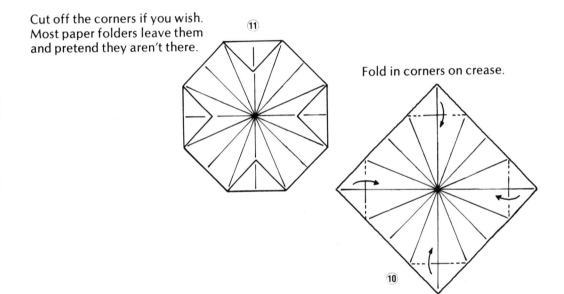

Cut off the corners if you wish.
Most paper folders leave them
and pretend they aren't there.

⑪

Fold in corners on crease.

⑩

Fold tips up over edge of paper.

Unfold completely.

⑧

⑨

Squash other three flaps.

123

Pinwheel or Zinnia Flower

Mr. Rohm called it a pinwheel and Mr. Kasahara thinks it is a flower Everybody thinks it is pretty enough to be a Christmas ornament. This best made from foil paper.

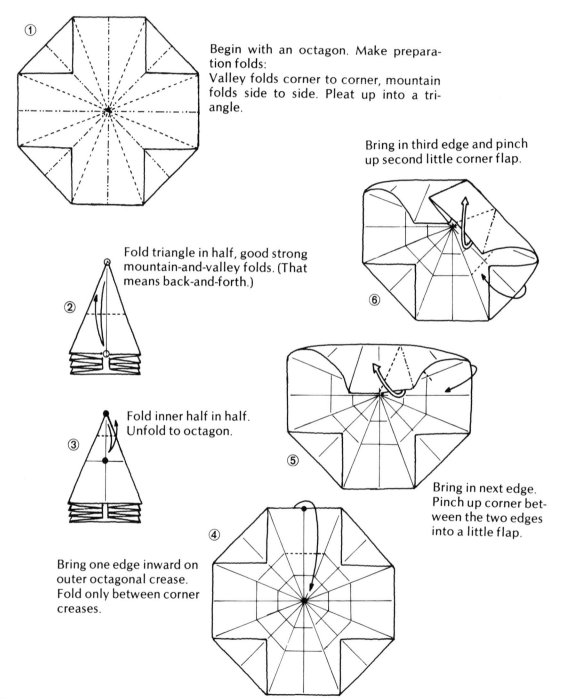

① Begin with an octagon. Make preparation folds:
Valley folds corner to corner, mountain folds side to side. Pleat up into a triangle.

Bring in third edge and pinch up second little corner flap.

⑥

② Fold triangle in half, good strong mountain-and-valley folds. (That means back-and-forth.)

③ Fold inner half in half. Unfold to octagon.

⑤ Bring in next edge. Pinch up corner between the two edges into a little flap.

④ Bring one edge inward on outer octagonal crease. Fold only between corner creases.

by Fred Rohm, U.S.A.

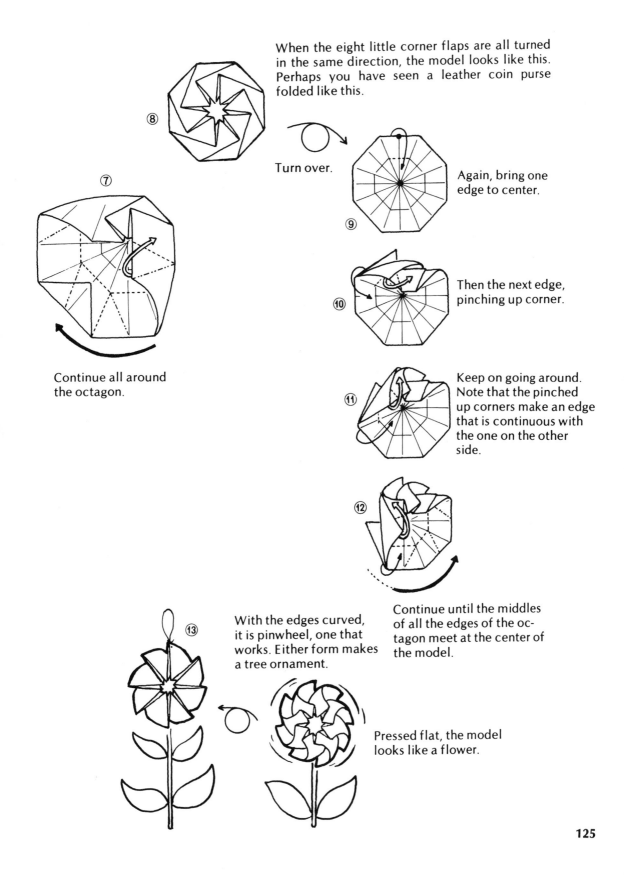

When the eight little corner flaps are all turned in the same direction, the model looks like this. Perhaps you have seen a leather coin purse folded like this.

⑧

Turn over.

⑨ Again, bring one edge to center.

⑦

Continue all around the octagon.

⑩ Then the next edge, pinching up corner.

⑪ Keep on going around. Note that the pinched up corners make an edge that is continuous with the one on the other side.

⑫ Continue until the middles of all the edges of the octagon meet at the center of the model.

⑬ With the edges curved, it is pinwheel, one that works. Either form makes a tree ornament.

Pressed flat, the model looks like a flower.

How to Make a Paper Circular

You can't do this by folding and cutting. The best way is to draw your circle with compass and cut it out with scissors. Or, draw around something that is round. With luck, you may find some round origami paper in book or toy shop.

Rocking Bird

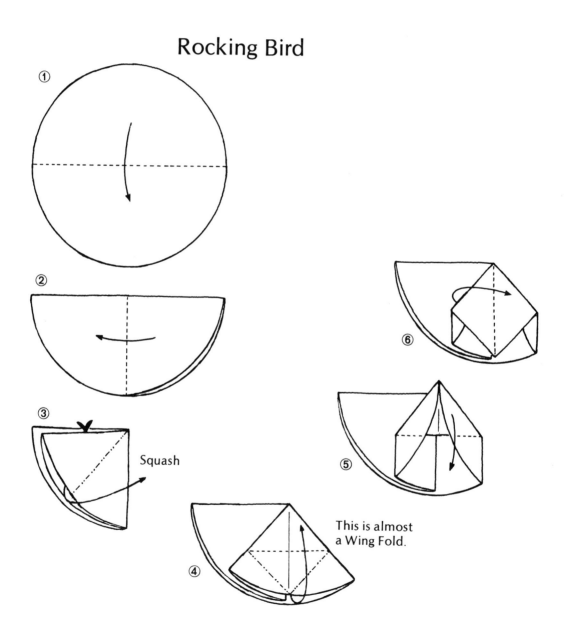

③ Squash

④ This is almost a Wing Fold.

by Kunihiko Kasahara

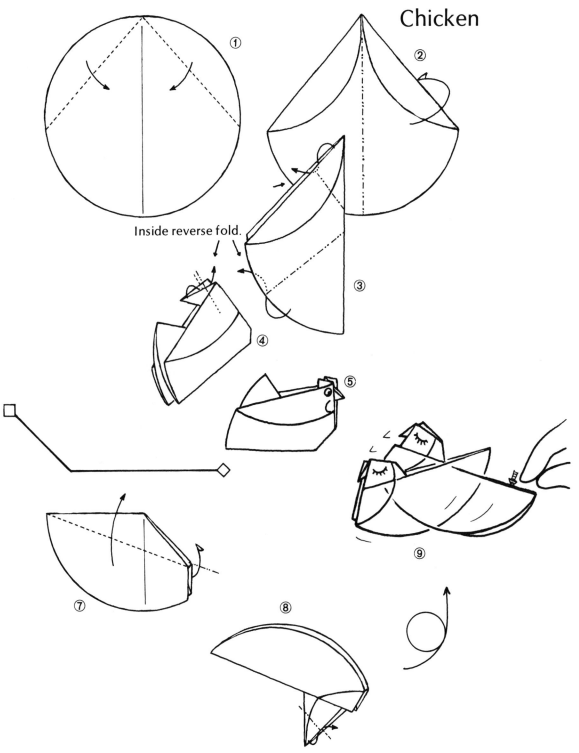

Chicken

① ② ③

Inside reverse fold.

④ ⑤ ⑦ ⑧ ⑨

Inside reverse fold.

by Kunihiko Kasahara

Nun

Use paper black on one side, white on the other.

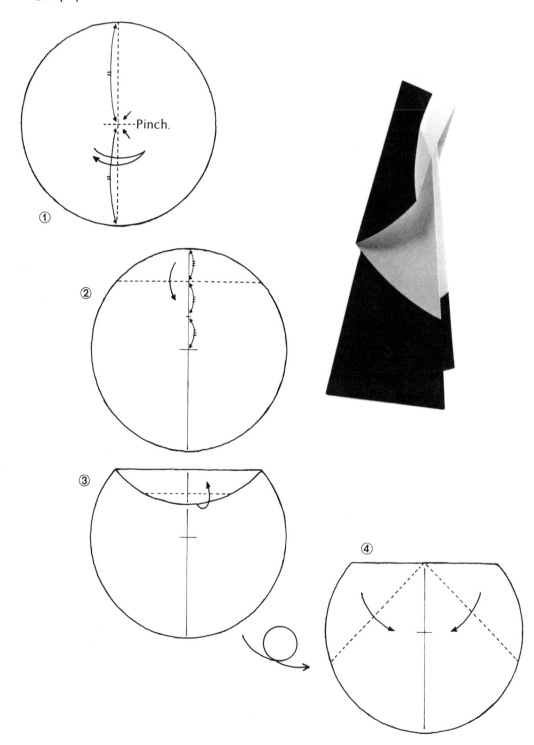

① Pinch.

②

③

④

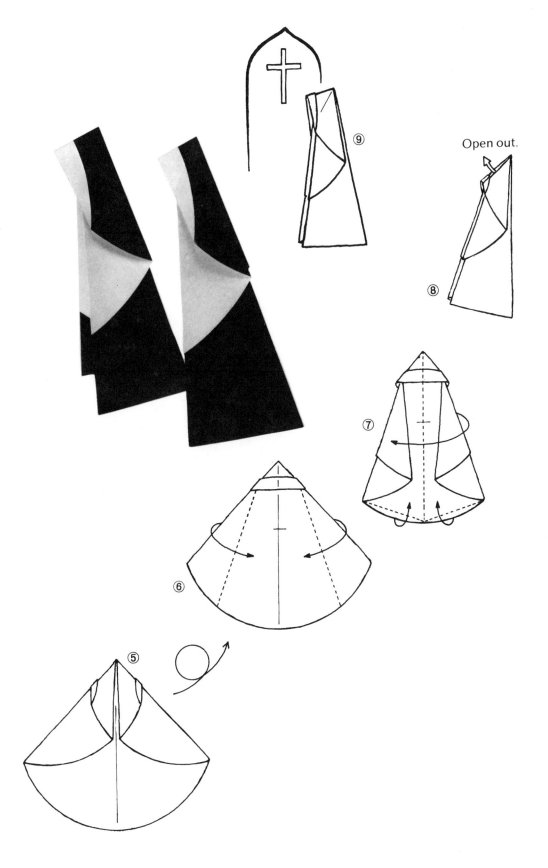

⑨

Open out.

⑧

⑦

⑥

⑤

129

by George Rhoads, U.S.A.

Invent Your Own Origami

Inventing your own origami is even more fun than folding things other people have invented. There are at least two way of doing it. The first just happens. You'll be folding something, and all at once it looks like something else. So, you'll change it a little, to make it look more like that something else. Presto! An invention! The second way is harder. You decide what you'd like to make, find out what it ought to look like, and then think how to go about making it. The more things you can already do with paper, the easier it will be to think how to make the model you want. The best folders work this way. Some of them say that the answer comes to them in a dream. If they don't get up and make the model right away, they lose it! By the time you have finished this book, you should be pretty good at inventing origami. When you have made something you like, you'll be proud of yourself, and you should. If, later, you find out that somebody else invented the same thing first, don't feel bad. It happens all the time. What you have done is no less yours because somebody else has done it too.

HAPPY FOLDING!

Index

alligator, 82
animal head finger puppet, 40

basic form, 14
basket, 26, 72
bed, 62
bird base, 14, 84
blintz base, 69
blow-top, 67
book fold, 14
boomerang plane, 22
boot, 29
bow-tie, 30
box, 24
boxer, 76
bride, 58

camera, 70
catamaran, 64
cat boat, 51
catcher's mitt, 18
chair, 63
chiken, 127
Christmas tree, 110, 112
Christmas tree ornament, 98
clown, 52
coaster, 56
crab, 50
crane, 84
crease, 11
crown, 68
crystal tree ornament, 102
cupboard-door fold, 14

diamond base, 50
diamond-shaped ornament, 101
diaper fold, 14
dog, 41
dory, 23
drop-shaped ornament, 104
dwarf, 44

eight sided solid, 119
eight vaned tree ornament, 103
elephant, 34
embroidered ball, 108
equilateral triangle, 116

faceted water-bomb, 75
fish base, 14, 80

five-pointed star, 120
flapping bird, 86
flapping crane, 86
flying wings, 38
fox, 41
frog, 92
frog base, 14
furniture, 25

ice-cream cone fold, 14
inside reverse fold, 13
iris, 94

jumping frog, 96

lily base, 14
leaping frog
lemon-shaped ornament, 105
letterfold, 20
lily, 94
lover's knot move
lucky crane, 85

model, 11
money fold, 30
mountain fold, 8
mouse, 115

napkin fold, 28, 29
needle case, 20
nodding bird, 43
nun, 128
nurse's cap, 19

octahedron, 107, 119
origami mobile, 79
orizuru, 84
ornamental ball, 109
outside-inside ornament, 101
outside reverse fold, 13

pentagon, 120
petal fold, 15
pig, 41
pigeon, 42
pinwheel, 64, 124
pop star, 87
preparation fold, 24
purse, 60
purse with latch, 60

rabbit, 28, 41, 90
rabbit ear, 12
rectangle, 18
regular hexagon, 118
regular octagon, 122
reverse fold, 13
ring, 32
rocking bird, 126

Santa Claus, 54
scallop shell, 49
sea shell, 48
shuttle fold, 25
six water-bomb base ornament, 78
snail, 88
square, how to make, 36
square ornament with shelves, 100
squashing, 12
stamp case, 60
star, 121
star of David, 117
stirrup ornament, 103
strawberry ornament, 104

table, 65
three-piece ornament, 46
tulip flower, 76
tumbler, 61
two-piece helicopter, 66
two-piece windmill, 67

umbrella, 122

valentine letter fold, 81
valley fold, 8

walking penguin, 37
wall clock, 63
water-bomb base, 14
water-bomb base and balloon, 74
windmill base, 64
wing fold, 15

x-ray view, 9

zig-zag tree ornament, 106
zinnia flower, 124